AF387960

Bomber Crew Escaper

Bomber Crew Escaper

One Wartime Airman's Story of Bailing Out, Capture, Imprisonment and Escape

Ian Richardson

First published in Great Britain in 2026
by Air World
An imprint of
Pen & Sword Books Limit
Yorkshire – Philadelphia

ISBN: 978 1 03618 178 9

Typeset in INDIA by IMPEC eSolutions
Printed and bound in UK by CPI Group (UK) Ltd, Croydon, CR0 4YY

The Publisher's authorised representative in the EU for product safety is Authorised Rep Compliance Ltd., Ground Floor, 71 Lower Baggot Street, Dublin D02 P593, Ireland
www.arccompliance.com

For a complete list of Pen & Sword titles please contact:

PEN & SWORD BOOKS LIMITED
47 Church Street, Barnsley, South Yorkshire, S70 2AS, England
E-mail: enquiries@pen-and-sword.co.uk
Website: www.pen-and-sword.co.uk

or

PEN AND SWORD BOOKS,
1950 Lawrence Road, Havertown, PA 19083, USA
E-mail: Uspen-and-sword@casematepublishers.com
Website: www.penandswordbooks.com

Contents

Introduction

222419 was the Prisoner of War number of 1580027 Sergeant Jack Sowter. He joined the RAFVR, in October 1941, as a trainee radio observer but, later, re-mustered as a navigator. Like countless others, entry into the Service was at the hallowed Lords Cricket Ground.

After the Air Crew Receiving Centre, he was posted to No. 3 Initial Training Wing at Torquay, and while there witnessed a Messerschmitt Bf 109 'hit and run' raider bomb and sink the vessel which was used as a boom across the harbour entrance.

From ITW he was posted to Empire Air Navigation School at Eastbourne, and after fleeting spells at West Kirby, Heaton Park and Blackpool, plus an aborted overseas posting, flying training began at Air Navigation School, Dumfries, where he was awarded his navigator wing.

His Operational Training Unit was at Lossiemouth where, with the exception of the flight engineer, the crew was formed with which Jack Sowter was destined to fly. It was at the Conversion Unit at Marston Moor where the crew was joined by the flight engineer. The crew's operations, until the fateful night of 27 July 1943 on Operation *Gomorrah*, were with 78 Squadron, 4 Group, based at Breighton.

Following his dramatic escapes and his eventual return to England, Jack Sowter was posted, initially, to Church Fenton followed by Marston Moor and then to the Transport Command Development Unit based at Harwell and Brize Norton, from which station he was demobilized in February 1946.

He wrote the story of his experiences in the aftermath of the bombing of Hamburg and the crashing of his plane. But his account began with only a brief preamble, starting as his aircraft lifted off on Operation *Gomorrah*. This was one of the most devastating air raids of the Second World War and to put Jack's tale into context, I have drawn on official British records to describe the planning of the operation and its effectiveness, and on official German reports from those on the ground who survived the horrifying firestorm. Part Two of this book is Jack's unabridged account of his time as a prisoner of war and his daring escape attempts. So devastating was the Hamburg raid that when, in captivity, it was seen that Jack was a flyer, he was physically attacked by a civilian, and called a '*Schweinehund*'.

Together, the stories of the horrors of the raid and of Jack's survival in captivity and his determination to break free from the clutches of his captors present a deeply personal side of the war through the words of those who fought and endured history's deadliest conflict.

Ian Richardson

PART ONE

THE BATTLE OF HAMBURG

Chapter 1

The Devastation of Hamburg – Operation Gomorrah: Preparation

The city of Hamburg was the second city of Germany and the greatest port in continental Europe. With a population of over 1.5 million before the war, it contained U-boat, aircraft and oil targets of the first importance, as well as every other major war industry. The main built up area was on the north of the River Elbe, while the port area lay mainly to the south. The principal industries were situated in the port area and round the perimeter of the main city area; Harburg was part of greater Hamburg, lying to the south of the main dock area. The attacks made upon Hamburg in the early months of 1943 were in preparation for the Battle of Hamburg. The following extracts illustrate the intention:

> The total destruction of this city would achieve immeasurable results in reducing the industrial capacity of the enemy's war machine ... The Battle of Hamburg cannot be won in a single night. It is estimated that at least 10,000 tons of bombs will have to be dropped to complete the process of elimination. To achieve the maximum effect of air bombardment this city should be subjected to sustained attack ... On the first attack a large number of incendiaries are to be carried in order to saturate the Fire Services.

This 'battle' was to place between 24 July and 3 August 1943. Bomber Command's Air Vice Marshal Sir Arthur Harris issued the following order which made his objectives very clear:

BOMBER COMMAND OPERATION ORDER NO. 173
Copy No: 23

Date: 27th May, 1943

INFORMATION

1. The importance of HAMBURG, the second largest city in Germany with a population of one and a half millions, is well known and needs no further emphasis. The total destruction of this city would achieve immeasurable results in reducing the industrial capacity of the enemy's war machine. This, together with the effect on German morale, which would be felt throughout the country, would play a very important part in shortening and in winning the war.

2. The 'Battle of Hamburg' cannot be won in a single night. It is estimated that at least 10,000 tons of bombs will have to be dropped to complete the process of elimination. To achieve the maximum effect of air bombardment, this city should be subjected to sustained attack.

Forces to be Employed:

3. Bomber Command forces will consist of all available heavies in operational squadrons until sufficient hours of darkness enable the medium bombers to take part. It is hoped that the night attacks will be preceded and/or followed by heavy daylight attacks by the United States VIIIth Bomber Command.

INTENTION

4. To destroy HAMBURG.[1]

---

[1] The National Archives, Air 24/257, Bomber Command Intelligence Reports.

Two new factors were to be employed. The development of H2S and experience gained in its use in the preceding months enabled a target situated against water, such as this, to be accurately marked by Pathfinders. The use of Window to counter the enemy radar defences reduced the loss rate to very small dimensions.

H2S had been used as a navigational aid and target marking device by Pathfinders since the night of 30/31 January 1943. Owing to inexperience in its use and various difficulties encountered it had not at first given much improved results. But its use made possible the outstanding success of the Hamburg raids. Very few H2S nets were available during the first two months of its use. The average was thirteen per raid, but poor serviceability reduced the effective number to about five. This difficulty was aggravated by bad timing of the Pathfinder and Main Force aircraft, and by the absence of long-burning Target Indicators. Those used burned for only about 2.5 minutes. A single badly-placed Target Indicator could therefore mislead the whole force. The need for more H2S equipped aircraft to mark the target was imperative.

As a navigational aid H2S was found to be highly satisfactory. Difficulties arose, however, in its operation over the target area. Poor definition and gaps in the polar diagram limited positive identification, whilst the effect of evasive action made the picture very difficult to interpret. The definition was improved by fitting a limiter, to reduce contrast on the PPI, and a wave guide scanner, giving a narrower beam, removing extraneous objects and filling up gaps. The addition of a roll-stabiliser to the scanner overcame the difficulties due to evasive action.

Overcoming these early troubles took considerable time. Both the number of H2S aircraft available and the timing of raids gradually improved, modifications to the sets took four to five months of experiment and manufacture, and a similar time lag was needed for the provision of long-burning Target Indicators.

At the same time bombing techniques with H2S were being developed. The tendency to undershoot was countered by orders to the backers-up to overshoot and it was found that the greatest success was still obtained by the laying of flares by H2S, so that the target could be visually checked by selected backers-up. The tendency to faulty identification at night had caused the suspension of this method for a time. By the end of July sufficient experience had been gained, and enough HS2 aircraft were available to ensure an accurate concentration upon Hamburg.

The use of 'Window' had been under consideration for a considerable period. This was a mechanical means of producing misleading echoes on radar apparatus by means of strips of aluminium dropped from aircraft. Difficulties of quantity production, and above all, fear of enemy retaliation in kind had prohibited its use up to 1943. On 3 May the Chiefs of Staff Committee considered an Air Staff memorandum advocating its use. In urging that the slight risks entailed were justified in view of the resulting increase in striking power, the Chief of the Air Staff said that some 455 bombers and their crews should be saved in the first eight months. This would not only build up the strength of the bomber force but would also increase its average of experience and therefore of efficiency. This would still further reduce losses and greatly improve morale.

The COS approved the use of Window from 1 July 1943, subject to technical examination of its implications, especially upon the launching of Operation *Husky*, the invasion of Sicily. The ad hoc sub-committee which examined the question reported on 11 May. They considered that the success of *Husky* should not be endangered by the use of Window before that operation had been launched. The target date was set at 1 July, with the intention of temporary postponement after that date as the progress of *Husky* should require. Bomber Command were therefore informed of this provisional date.

In the instruction for its use issued by Bomber Command on 17 July 1943, all heavy and medium operational squadrons were ordered to be ready to discharge it by 23 July 1943. It was only to be discharged on the occasions and at the rates ordered by Bomber Command. The optimum rate of discharge was estimated at one bundle per minute per aircraft for a concentration of 600 aircraft per hour. Rates of dropping for use in orders were laid down, from Rate A, one bundle per two minutes, to Rate E, three per minute. On occasion 350 to 400lb of Window would have to be carried in each aircraft. Care had to be taken not to stow it too far aft of the centre of gravity. A height concentration of 6,000 feet would be required; aircraft must fly within 3,000 feet of the height specified.

As Window was only effective against RDF apparatus, its discharge was to be limited to those areas where known GCI or GL stations were sited, or enemy fighters equipped with Aircraft Interception (AI) radar. A map of these areas was prepared, and Window was to be discharged while traversing them. Regular spacing was important, and the crew member releasing Window – the air bomber or Wireless Operator were suggested – must be provided with a watch.

Window was first used on 24/25 July 1943 in the first of the big attacks upon Hamburg. It was used only against Würzburgs, which were used for GCI control and gunlaying. The system of control was immediately thrown into confusion, and new expedients had to be sought by the enemy to bring their fighters into contact with the bomber stream. Later types of Window were devised for use against all known forms of enemy radar.

One further countermeasure was introduced during the Battle of Hamburg; this was Ground Cigar, which jammed the VHF/RT frequencies beginning to be employed by enemy night fighters. A transmitter had been set up at Sizewell on the Suffolk coast to operate a jamming barrage over the whole waveband employed. It came into operation on 30/31 July 1943.

Chapter 2

Advance to Target

The first bomber to take off on July 24 was an old Stirling from No. 75 (New Zealand) Squadron which left the ground at 9.45 p.m. The night began with an incident that foreshadowed the dangers ahead. Among the hundreds of heavy bombers preparing to depart, one Halifax suffered a troubled start. Its first attempt to take off ended abruptly when an engine cut out. The pilot managed to brake in time, preventing the fully loaded aircraft from overshooting the runway. After a brief consultation among the crew, the engines were checked and the pilot prepared for a second attempt. As the Halifax lifted from the ground the two outer engines lost power, causing a sudden loss of thrust at the most critical moment. The pilot steered away from the control caravan at the end of the runway, burst through the boundary fence, and skidded into the adjoining field. The aircraft carried two target indicators and four heavy high-explosive bombs, any of which could have detonated on impact. Quick action by the pilot and engineer shut off the fuel, cut the magnetos, and triggered the fire-extinguishing system. Expecting an explosion, the crew scattered across the dark field, only to realize moments later that the bomber would not ignite. Relief swept through them and they laughed nervously at their escape. Remarkably, no one was injured.

This accident was the only mishap during take-off. Soon afterward the night's operation gathered full momentum. One by one the last of 791 bombers roared down the runways of forty-two airfields, their departure times carefully calculated so that the massive force would converge over the sea in an organized stream. Groups left from different points along the English coast, each assigned a particular departure path to prevent confusion as the long procession formed over the dark waters. Spirits among the aircrews were higher than on most operations. Many were weary of the endless raids against the same industrial region of western Germany, a repetitive task that had come to be described as little more than turning over rubble. This mission offered a change – a longer flight over open water and a target in a distant part of the country. There was also the knowledge that this raid marked the start of a concentrated series of attacks intended to obliterate a major city. At their briefings earlier in the day, crews had been told that a new countermeasure against enemy radar would be used for the first time. It involved the dropping of countless bundles of thin, metallic strips designed to create false echoes on radar screens. Some of the more experienced men were sceptical, but all understood the importance of the experiment.

As the bombers climbed steadily over the North Sea, the weight of their full bomb loads tested engines and airframes. Mechanical troubles soon began to claim a share of the force. Forty-five aircraft turned back before reaching the enemy coast, an attrition rate of roughly 6 per cent – typical for a raid of this magnitude. Lancaster bombers proved the most reliable, with only a small percentage returning early, while Halifaxes suffered the highest proportion of failures. One Halifax attempting to return after an engine malfunction crash-landed at its home airfield, but again the crew escaped unharmed. Apart from these setbacks, conditions for flying were excellent. A layer of low cloud covered the sea, but above it the night was clear, the stars sharp in the cold upper air. Navigators received reliable fixes from the Gee radio-navigation system until the signals began to weaken roughly 300 miles from England. Enemy jamming started late and targeted the wrong network of transmitters, leaving many crews able to obtain fixes throughout the flight. The light northerly wind posed no significant challenge to navigation. The aircraft climbed gradually toward operational heights of 15–18,000 feet, still gaining altitude as they approached the enemy coast. Their instruments showed an indicated airspeed of around 160 miles per hour, though the true speed in the thin upper air exceeded 200 miles per hour. Darkness deepened across the sea; the moon had not yet risen. Most crews saw little of the other aircraft despite the vast numbers in the sky, only the occasional flicker of exhaust flames betraying the presence of other bombers far below.

The enemy's defensive network received its first warning well before the bombers reached the coast. Radar stations along the continental shoreline detected the approaching stream and passed reports up the chain of command. Controllers in Holland and northern Germany recognized that the British force might once again be heading for the industrial valleys to the south, a frequent target in recent months. Fighter groups were ordered to prepare for interception, with night fighters climbing into the darkness to occupy their assigned patrol zones along the coast. As the bombers continued eastward without turning south, the fighter divisions guarding the approaches to the night's true objective were also alerted. All of this took place before the first bundles of radar-confusing strips began to flutter from the lead aircraft.

While the bomber force advanced, a small number of fast twin-engined aircraft of the British fighter command undertook diversionary operations against enemy airfields. Weather concerns over southern England, including the possibility of fog later in the night, led to the cancellation of most of these intruder sorties. Only a handful took off, and all but one were recalled. A single aircraft pressed on alone, reaching an enemy night-fighter base on a northern island. There it intercepted a German plane that was taking off with navigation lights still visible. The British crew opened fire and destroyed the fighter, which crashed into the sea. This skirmish occurred shortly before midnight, when the leading bombers were still some distance from the enemy coast, and it proved to be the only intruder success of the night.

The main bomber force soon entered the defensive zones off the northern coast of Holland where enemy fighters waited for an expected turn toward the Ruhr. Some combats took place here, but the first encounters were brief and inconclusive. In each case the vigilant gunners of the bombers spotted the attackers first, and the fighters broke away without scoring hits. Two bombers, however, drifted far off the designated route and became easy prey for the tightly controlled interception system. One enemy pilot shot down a Lancaster with a single burst of fire, sending it straight into the sea. Another bomber, also off course, was destroyed in a similar fashion. The positions of these losses suggest that both aircraft had suffered mechanical problems and were attempting to return to the English coast when they were caught. Their crews were lost without trace. These incidents demonstrated the efficiency of the enemy's radar-guided boxes, which could quickly destroy any straggler separated from the main stream.

Far out over the sea, the bomber navigators worked to bring their aircraft into the designated assembly point where the separate routes from England converged. On their charts this was marked as a fixed position 80 miles from the first landfall on the German coast. Here the massive bomber stream would finally form before pressing on toward the target. In theory the stream was planned to be more than 200 miles long, based on the scheduled duration of the bombing and the expected speed of the aircraft over the city. The plan envisioned a neatly organized procession, each aircraft holding its course and speed with precision. In practice the formation resembled an irregular mass, each crew striving to maintain the assigned track but with inevitable deviations caused by the difficulties of dead-reckoning navigation in darkness.

Five minutes beyond the assembly point, the leading bombers began releasing the first bundles of metallic strips. Scientists had calculated that at a distance of 35 miles from the enemy coast, the Würzburg radar stations controlling the night-fighter boxes became fully effective. Each bundle contained thousands of narrow strips that scattered into a slowly descending cloud, creating a radar echo resembling that of a bomber. The cloud remained effective for at least fifteen minutes before dispersing. Every aircraft was instructed to drop one bundle per minute until reaching the same distance from the coast on the return journey two hours later. At this early stage the responsibility for releasing the strips varied from crew to crew. Some squadrons assigned the task to the flight engineer, others to the wireless operator or bomb aimer. In a few cases the mid–upper gunner was chosen, a decision that left one of the defensive turrets unoccupied during the most dangerous part of the flight. The designated crew member worked alone in the cold, dark fuselage, using a torch and stopwatch to push the bundles through a chute or hatch at precise intervals. It was an uncomfortable and unpopular duty, but essential to the night's success.

Minor mishaps were common. Some crewmen struggled to force the bulky bundles through narrow chutes, resorting to boots or other objects to push them free. Others accidentally dropped personal items or lost track of their timing equipment in the darkness. The black coating on one side of the strips rubbed off easily, staining clothing and even the Perspex of gun turrets. Yet these inconveniences did not prevent the majority of aircraft from maintaining a steady stream of radar decoys. The results soon exceeded all expectations.

Within twenty minutes of the first release, the bomber stream was flying through several of the main night-fighter boxes along the coast. Normally these heavily defended zones would have guided fighters with precision onto the bombers. Now the German controllers faced radar screens flooded with false targets. For every genuine echo there were numerous phantom returns, and during some periods the descending strips created such confusion that fighter direction had to be abandoned altogether. British wireless operators, monitoring the enemy control frequencies, reported a rising tone of agitation as orders became contradictory and interceptions failed. Ground controllers transmitted frantic instructions, but their fighters were chasing ghosts scattered across the sky.

The enemy's difficulty in controlling its fighters allowed the bomber stream to cross the outer defensive belt almost unopposed. The first radar boxes guarding the approaches to the target lay on the islands of Sylt and Heligoland, where powerful stations had been tracking the approaching force for some time. Normally these sites would have been among the most dangerous obstacles, reaching far out to sea in an effort to strike the head of an incoming formation before it reached the mainland. On this night their radars detected the stream clearly, but the cloud of metallic strips rendered the precision tracking sets useless. Interceptors patrolling the north-western edges of these boxes searched in vain for targets as the bombers slipped past.

While the enemy ground controllers struggled with the deceptive echoes, the leading British aircraft continued their duties. Beyond the radar-confusing clouds, six Pathfinder crews prepared to mark the route for the force behind them. Each carried special bombs packed with dozens of bright pyrotechnic candles. At the exact moment their radar screens showed the outline of the coast crossing the centre of the display, they released the markers. Bursting at a pre-set height, the bombs scattered a cascade of brilliant yellow lights that drifted slowly toward the ground in a long chain of golden sparks. Visible for miles across the dark sea, these route markers indicated the precise point where the bomber stream should tighten its formation after the long crossing over the featureless North Sea. Other Pathfinders followed at intervals to renew the markers and ensure that the tail of the stream could follow the same course.

The coastline selected for this dramatic display lay on a small peninsula of Schleswig, well south of the Danish border though many airmen would later describe it mistakenly as Denmark. Letters and diaries from the crews frequently referred to incidents over Denmark or the Danish coast despite clear markings on their maps. To the men in the cockpits, anything north of Hamburg seemed Danish, a small geographical inaccuracy that persisted long after the event. Two bombers experiencing mechanical problems used this opportunity to release their bombs as soon as they crossed the coast. Dropping their loads on enemy soil allowed the crews to claim a completed operational flight despite being unable to reach the main target. One person on the ground was killed by these early jettisoned bombs.

The bright route markers inevitably attracted enemy attention. Observation posts reported the display to higher headquarters, and the message was relayed to all nearby fighter units. Night fighters already patrolling the area also saw the lights and began searching for bomber targets. For thirty minutes, however, nothing happened. More than 500 bombers passed safely over the coast while the markers were steadily renewed. Then at last an enemy fighter scouting seaward of the lights intercepted a bomber. A long burst of cannon fire brought the aircraft down in flames above the sea, where it broke apart before striking the water. This Halifax, flying in the fifth wave of the attack, was the only bomber destroyed at the coast itself. The identity of the German pilot remains uncertain.

Another combat followed shortly afterward when a Halifax on its first operation came under attack from directly astern. The tail gunner responded instantly, and the fighter plunged away in a steep dive trailing fire. It was later believed that the attacker was a Dornier night fighter that crashed while attempting to return to base, its crew partly lost. This small British victory brought brief satisfaction to the novice crew, though their success was short-lived. They completed three more operations in the next five nights but were later shot down into the sea not far from the site of their initial encounter, with no survivors.

The bomber stream pressed on toward its next turning point, 27 miles north-west of the target city. Along the route some crews released leaflets over German towns, part of the ongoing psychological campaign. Flak batteries and searchlights became more active as the force approached the Kiel Canal, a heavily defended stretch that crews disliked crossing. The canal was protected by dense concentrations of anti-aircraft guns and powerful searchlights capable of trapping a bomber in a cone of light for the gunners to aim at. Here another bomber met its end. A slower Stirling, flying below the altitude of the more powerful aircraft, was caught in the beams and heavily engaged by flak. In attempting to evade the lights the pilot left the protective bomber stream and the cover of the radar-confusing strips. An enemy night fighter soon detected the isolated aircraft and finished it off. Three of the crew managed to parachute to safety, becoming the first prisoners of the night.

Flight Sergeant F.H. Tritton of 100 Squadron was on his first operational flight: 'I remember, on the outward journey, how forlorn I felt, wondering what lay ahead and feeling queasy in the stomach but at the same time determined to put on a brave front with these hardened veterans I was flying with. It was when we were flying south over the Kiel Canal that certain changes came over the crew. The breathing over the intercom, which before had been fairly measured, now became quickened and loudened quite considerably; the speech became very clipped and, at odd moments, tempers were obviously rather frayed.'[2]

Another brief encounter occurred when a Stirling exchanged fire with a fighter identified as a single-engine interceptor, but the combat ended without damage to either side. For the most part, however, the entire bomber stream – over 200 miles long and containing more than 700 aircraft – passed through the northern defensive boxes with remarkably light losses. Only two bombers were destroyed on or near the planned route across the coast, and it is likely that none of these

---

[2] Martin Middlebrook, *The Battle of Hamburg, The Firestorm Raid* (Penguin, London, 1988), p.133.

successes resulted from a standard ground-controlled interception. The new radar countermeasure had already proved its value.

Nevertheless, the protective strips could not save aircraft that strayed far from the stream. Two Halifaxes flying well to the north provided typical examples of the danger. One, 30 miles off course near Schleswig, was intercepted by a night fighter whose pilot scored his first victory of the war. Another, 60 miles from the main track but flying the correct heading, was caught near the Danish border and shot down. Both were inexperienced crews undertaking their first or second operations.

Despite these scattered losses, the bomber stream held together remarkably well as it neared the enemy coastline. On every navigator's chart was a critical point known simply as Position A, located 80 miles from the landfall on the German coast. This was the place where all the separate routes from England converged and where the bomber stream finally assembled for its run to the target. The position lay 290 miles from the English bases and was reached by the leading aircraft about twenty minutes after midnight. From this point onward the plan envisioned a stream extending more than 200 miles, based on the scheduled fifty-three-minute duration of the raid and the estimated speed of the bombers over the city. Theoretical calculations imagined a neat procession of aircraft flying at exactly the same speed along the same track, though at different heights suited to each type. In practice, of course, the stream was an irregular mass of aircraft maintaining roughly the same course and speed but with inevitable variations caused by the difficulties of night navigation.

As the leading aircraft crossed this assembly point, the first bundles of radar-confusing strips began to drift down into the darkness. Scientists had chosen this position carefully, believing it to be the point at which the enemy's coastal radars became fully effective. Each bundle contained thousands of slender, metallized strips that would flutter to earth at a rate of several hundred feet per minute, producing a radar echo indistinguishable from that of a heavy bomber. The effect lasted at least fifteen minutes, enough to create a moving corridor of false targets through which the stream could safely pass. Every aircraft was instructed to release one bundle per minute until it reached the equivalent distance from the coast on the homeward journey. The task of dropping the strips fell to different crew members depending on squadron preference: flight engineers in some cases, wireless operators or bomb aimers in others. A few units even assigned the mid-upper gunner, a choice that left one of the defensive turrets unmanned during the most hazardous part of the flight. Whoever performed the duty worked in darkness with a torch and stopwatch, pushing the bundles through a chute or hatch at precise intervals while the bomber roared through the freezing night.

Handling the strips was far from pleasant. The bundles were bulky and sometimes jammed in the narrow chutes, forcing crewmen to use boots or other objects to push them clear. Some accidentally dropped personal items along with the strips, while others lost track of their timing equipment in the gloom. The black coating on one side of the strips rubbed off easily, staining faces, hands, and even the Perspex of gun turrets. By the time they returned to England many men resembled coal miners despite their oxygen masks and heavy clothing. Yet these discomforts did nothing to diminish the success of the tactic. The false echoes multiplied across the enemy radar screens, overwhelming the control officers with a blizzard of spurious targets and rendering their night-fighter boxes virtually blind.

While the enemy struggled to make sense of the multiplying echoes on their screens, the bomber stream advanced toward the final leg of its journey. The city chosen as the night's target lay beside a great river estuary on the north German plain, a vital port and industrial centre of immense strategic value. For years it had been spared the relentless pounding suffered by other German cities. Only scattered raids had touched it, and many of its citizens still believed that geography or fortune might protect them. That illusion would end within the hour.

The plan for the attack was carefully constructed. The first wave consisted of Pathfinder crews whose job was to mark the aiming point with coloured target indicators. Behind them came a succession of main-force waves, each scheduled to arrive at precise intervals so that the bombing could continue without pause for more than fifty minutes. This method ensured that the enemy's civil defences would be overwhelmed and that fires would have no chance to be contained before the next weight of bombs fell. Navigators checked their watches against the carefully prepared timetable as they guided their aircraft through the final turning points. Pilots monitored their altitude and speed with constant attention, conscious that any deviation might separate them from the protective stream and the cascading clouds of radar-confusing strips.

The bomber stream continued its long, dark approach to the target, the aircraft now fully committed to the final stage of their mission. The great armada of heavy bombers – spread across more than 200 miles of night sky – pressed steadily toward the city that lay beyond the Elbe. Below, the landscape of northern Germany revealed only sparse points of light, most towns already darkened by blackout regulations. The North Sea was now far behind, and the navigators tracked their progress by instruments and radar, carefully maintaining course despite the subtle drift of the northern winds. Though the stream appeared on paper as a tight, ordered procession, in reality it remained an irregular assembly of aircraft flying at slightly different heights and speeds, separated by varying distances but united in purpose.

As the bombers advanced, the enemy defences struggled to regain control. Radar operators in coastal stations attempted to separate the false echoes created by the strips of metallic foil that now filled the night air. The British had planned the deployment of these radar-confusing strips to perfection, ensuring that the German tracking network would be overwhelmed by countless phantom targets. Ground controllers sent urgent instructions to their night-fighter crews, but the confusion was complete. Fighters were directed to pursue contacts that did not exist, their radars showing blizzards of deceptive reflections. The tightly controlled interception system that normally allowed defenders to guide their aircraft to precise interception points was effectively blinded.

Despite the chaos, some enemy pilots managed to find their way toward the bomber stream. Sporadic combats broke out as isolated night fighters stumbled into the great moving column. Alert gunners in the bombers returned fire, sometimes driving off attackers before they could even open fire themselves. A few bombers were lost, but the attrition was far lower than would normally be expected on such a deep penetration. Window, as the new countermeasure was known, was proving its worth beyond the hopes of its creators. The crews, trained to drop bundles of the foil every minute, continued their routine with mechanical precision. Some worked from cramped flare chutes in the cold fuselage, timing their drops with stopwatches despite numb fingers and the discomfort of oxygen masks. Mishaps were inevitable: bundles jammed in chutes, small items were lost to the night sky, and some crew members emerged with faces blackened by the rubbing of the coated strips. Yet the vast majority of the radar-confusing clouds were released exactly as planned, forming a moving curtain of deception that left the defenders guessing.

Within the bomber stream, the tension was constant. Pilots maintained a steady climb toward operational height, throttles pushed to the limit as they coaxed their heavily laden aircraft through the thin upper air. The engines droned at maximum effort, their vibrations transmitted through every panel and rivet. Navigators hunched over their charts and instruments, watching for the next radar fix or the faint trace of coastline that would mark the approach to the target. Wireless operators listened on German frequencies, hearing fragments of frantic conversations from enemy controllers but refraining from their usual jamming duties so that the effects of the radar deception could be carefully assessed later. Gunners scanned the dark void for the faint silhouette of an approaching fighter or the sudden flash of tracer fire. Every man knew that at any moment the sky could erupt in lethal combat.

The leading Pathfinders were the first to sight the coastal peninsula that marked the next turning point. These specially trained crews released bright pyrotechnic markers to guide the main force, their bombs bursting into brilliant cascades of color that drifted slowly toward the ground. The spectacle was striking even at high altitude, a silent display of sparkling light that contrasted sharply with the blackness of the night. Behind them, the stream of bombers adjusted course, crowding into a tighter formation as they followed the luminous path across the featureless plain. The markers were renewed at intervals to maintain a continuous guide for the waves of aircraft still crossing the sea.

Some bombers experiencing mechanical problems took advantage of the proximity to land to jettison their loads over sparsely populated areas, ensuring that their flights would still be counted as operational despite the early return. Enemy observers on the ground reported the markers and passed the information up the chain of command, but the disorganized night-fighter system struggled to convert these reports into effective interceptions. Only after hundreds of aircraft had safely crossed the coast did the defenders begin to achieve isolated successes. A handful of bombers were picked off, some vanishing in sudden blossoms of flame, others limping away trailing smoke before plunging into the sea. Yet these losses were remarkably few compared to the scale of the attack.

The bomber stream pressed on toward the great city on the Elbe. Leaflets were released along the route, part of the ongoing psychological campaign intended to undermine civilian morale. Anti-aircraft defences grew heavier as the force approached the Kiel Canal, where concentrations of searchlights and flak batteries filled the sky with converging beams and exploding shells. The sudden brilliance of dozens of searchlights probing the night was a terrifying sight for the crews, who knew that once caught in the overlapping beams a bomber could become an easy target for the gunners below. One heavy bomber, slower and more vulnerable than most, was illuminated by a full cone of lights and subjected to intense fire. The pilot dived and twisted in a desperate attempt to escape but in doing so left the protective cover of the stream and the masking effect of the radar-confusing foil. A night fighter, guided by its own radar, soon intercepted and destroyed the isolated aircraft. Only a few of its crew survived to be taken prisoner.

Despite these isolated tragedies, the main force swept through the danger zones with surprisingly little loss. By the time the leading elements neared the final turning point north of the target, the bomber stream had passed through multiple layers of coastal and inland defences that would normally have claimed a far higher toll. The new countermeasures, combined with careful planning and the sheer weight of numbers, had carried the force to the very doorstep of the target almost intact.

Inside the defending command centres, frustration mounted. Reports from radar stations were contradictory, filled with phantom contacts and false trails. Controllers struggled to piece together a coherent picture from the overwhelming clutter, their efforts hampered by the deliberate radio silence of the attackers and the relentless interference of the metallic strips drifting slowly to earth. Fighter groups were shuffled from one sector to another in the hope of intercepting the intruders, but the speed and altitude of the bomber stream allowed it to outpace many of the attempted interceptions. Some German pilots later reported firing on targets that simply disappeared or chasing echoes that turned out to be nothing but drifting clouds of foil. The carefully constructed defensive system, long regarded as a formidable barrier, had been rendered nearly powerless.

As the force neared its objective, the city below lay under a thin layer of cloud illuminated faintly by the glow of the moon, which was now rising over the eastern horizon. The Pathfinders prepared to drop their first target indicators, the coloured flares that would mark the aiming points for the waves of bombers following behind. The success of the entire operation depended on their accuracy. Navigators watched the radar screens intently, searching for the distinctive outlines of the river and surrounding features that would confirm their position. Bomb aimers adjusted their sights, waiting for the precise moment to release their markers. Far behind, the main force readied their payloads, the great bomb bays filled with high explosives and incendiaries intended to devastate the industrial heart of the city.

The long journey across the sea and through the outer defences was almost complete. Despite mechanical failures, the occasional success of enemy fighters, and the ever-present threat of flak, the overwhelming majority of the attacking aircraft had reached the target area in good order. The next phase of the operation—the attack itself—was about to begin. The crews, tense but resolute, prepared for the deadly work ahead as their aircraft roared across the final miles of darkened countryside toward the city that would soon be engulfed in flame.

Chapter 3

The Horrors of the Hamburg Raid[3]

Fifteen-years-old Hans Erich Nossack leaped out of bed when he heard the heavy drone of incalculable numbers of heavy aircraft approaching. He had slept through the sirens as the wind was blowing the opposite direction. But there was no mistaking the sound of the RAF bombers: 'We had already experienced two hundred or even more air raids, among them some very heavy ones, but this was something completely new. And yet there was an immediate recognition: this was what everyone had been waiting for, what had hung for months like a shadow over everything we did, making us weary. It was the end. This sound was to last an hour and a half, and then again on three nights of the following week. It hung steadily in the air and remained steady even when the much louder din of the defence intensified to a drumfire. Only at moments when individual squadrons descended for a strafing did it swell and graze the earth with its wings. And yet this terrible noise was so permeable that every other sound could be heard as well: not just the reports of the antiaircraft guns, the bursting of grenades, the howling roar of bombs, the singing of shrapnel, no, even a very soft rustling, no louder than that of a withered leaf dropping from branch to branch, and for which there was no explanation in the darkness.[4]

---

[3] *The Hamburg Police President's Report on the Large Scale Air Attacks on Hamburg, Germany, in World War II.* [Translated version by Edith Müller Molton] Prepared by Carl F. Miller for Office of Civil Defense [and] Office of the Secretary of the Army, through Civil Defense Laboratory, 1968.

[4] Hans Erich Nossack, *The End: Hamburg 1943* (University of Chicago Press, London, 2004), p.8.

Kalix, Master of the Hamburg Security Police (No. 5142), submitted the following report on 25 August, regarding what he said was a rescue of persons from certain death of asphyxiation in an air raid shelter.

'During the night of July 24-25, 1943, in which the enemy brought untold horrors to our beautiful Hamburg. two of my colleagues in the police force and I were assigned to rescue endangered persons. After our precinct house had been damaged by high explosive and fire bombs to such an extent that the rescue of material possessions was out of the question, our police precinct personnel initiated actions to rescue residents from burning buildings and bring them to safety. Without cessation, we sent women and children hurrying through the streets to reach the Elevated Train Station at Emillienstrasse where there was comparative safety.

'A sergeant approached me and pointed out that about 150 persons had taken shelter in the Public Shelter at 136 Fruchtallee. The Heusshof was on fire, and the people in the shelter there needed to be checked on.

'Together with Reserve Master Sergeant Pourlenskl and my colleague Nordwald from our precinct, I left for the above-mentioned shelter. When we arrived, the second story of the Heusshof was on fire, but the occupants of the shelter located under the Heusshof did not seem to be in any danger. About 90 foreign workers of various nationalities were in the shelter, as well as about 60 German citizens, mostly older men and women and children. The lights had ceased to function. The German people in the shelter were hopeful that the air attack would soon be over and that they would be able to return to their apartments. The foreigners, on the other hand, were very restless, especially the Frenchmen. Our citizens, however, after being reassured by us, were not influenced by them. The responsible air-raid warden, Mr. Hahn, was constantly reassuring the people in the shelter.

'After we had ascertained that for the time being there was no danger to the shelter occupants, we went back out into the street where we resumed our previous task. I told the shelter inhabitants that we would keep an eye on them and would return if it became necessary. This explanation seemed especially reassuring to them.

'After a while, the fire in the Heusshof building was getting stronger so that the ground floor had begun to burn. Together with my comrades I again went to the building. By now it had become absolutely necessary to evacuate the shelter and to direct people to the Elevated Train Station at Emillienstrasse. The ceiling began to heat up, and through the air vent, fumes had begun to seep into the cellar. Worst of all, heavy smoke had begun to filter in. The emergency exit could not be used, because the wooden boards there were on fire. We decided to evacuate the cellar immediately to save the people from certain death by asphyxiation.

'The foreign workers were urged to pick up the children in their arms and to assist the women out of the shelter. Our orders were obeyed without question.

'All persons present were asked to use the centre of the street and get to the elevated station aa quickly as possible. Thus, the shelter was evacuated in a very short time. Now and then, there was a brief delay when the flames flared up in front of the cellar exit, but our women were very brave; they put cloths and blankets around their heads.

'My colleagues were tirelessly moving the people to the street. I remained in the cellar and supervised the departure. In the meantime, the fire increased in intensity. The movie house located next to the Heusshof had started to burn. Stay in the shelter became more and more intolerable. Sweat broke out all over my body, and my eyes burned from smoke and heat. I made the rounds of all the cellar rooms once more to make sure everyone was out. After receiving no answer any longer to my repeated calls, I left the shelter, presumably the last person to do so.

'I reached the outside only with the greatest difficulty because of the flames from above, especially since the exit at the cinema was blocked by a firewall. I gained the street by climbing over a collapsed wall.

'A short time before, Reserve Master Sergeant Pourlenski had used the same route with the last occupants of the shelter. We were overjoyed to be able to save these poor people. The air raid shelter itself withstood the attack and remained intact, but the people would have been killed by the intense heat. To my deep regret, I learned the next day from the air-raid warden, Mr. Hahn, that two bodies were found in the shelter. One was a Frenchman, and the other an elderly German citizen. They must have crawled away and remained in the cellar without our knowing it. I was not able to find anyone when I left the shelter; however, it was very dark and thick smoke had filled the rooms.'

Master Kalix explained that the evacuation of the shelter took place after the attack was over.

A member of the Reserve Security Police of the 30th Civil Defence Precinct, called Kumierczyk, provided his report on 6 September of the rescue of 280 people from the shelter Caffmacherreihe:

'During the night of July 24–25, 1943, I was in charge of the public air-raid shelter Caffamacherreihe 1/5, Industrial Palace. As soon as the alarm sounded, the shelter filled with 280 persons. These were mostly families with children and a few single persons. Strong flak fire had already begun, and I stayed at the door of the sluice to be able to survey the situation better. Suddenly, a fire was reported in the house Caffamacherreihe 28, and the emergency squad was alerted. I was in the process of opening the gas sluice, when suddenly a bomb (direct hit) dropped on the Industrial Palace. The air pressure lifted the sluice door from its hinges. The benches with the shelter occupants were thrown all over, and the electric lights went out. I immediately lit the reserve petroleum lamps and with the help of some brave men and with a forceful manner, I restored calm.

'Visibility in the room was zero, since the air was thick with a layer of dust. The entrance to the sluice was cut off by fallen masonry. I immediately checked the remaining exits, which led to the yard toward Caffamacherreihe and saw that these too were blocked by fallen masonry and wooden beams burning brightly. They could not be used.

'Now I went to the wall breakthrough that led to the open onto Speckstrasse and pushed this through. Here flames were thrown at me from the houses on Speckstrasse, and this way too was completely blocked at present. The stairs leading to this exit were removed by me since there wan danger that the wooden parts would catch fire. We were completely surrounded by fire on all sides and were forced to wait until we could find a way after the block of houses on Speckstrasse had burned down.

'Toward 9 p.m., this opportunity presented itself. After moving aside burning beams and masonry, an exit could be cleared toward Speckstrasse, and I was able to bring all persons to safety along this narrow path. The path that had to be cleared was about 100 meters long, and many persons had to be carried since they fainted from the intense heat. All present assisted one another and persons who showed signs of fainting were revived with water or other refreshment.

'The behaviour of all present was exemplary, and I did not note a single case of panic. The occupants completely entrusted themselves to me and my troup members, and there were no incidents. After I again checked all rooms thoroughly, I left the shelter as the last person.'

The squad leader of 1/IV Brigade of the Fire Protection Police, Stanowski, had just began a two-week period of recuperation leave when, on the night of 24-25 July, the air raid sirens began their nerve-shredding wail:

'During the air attack in the night, I went on the roof of my residence at Süderstrasse 319. The house, as well as surrounding buildings, was hit by stick firebombs. I extinguished two stick bombs and then ordered the self-protection service to look after things. In the back of the house at Süderstrasse 323, the rafters were on fire. I gave orders to several political leaders to form bucket chains and start fighting the fire. After I had the impression that I was no longer needed there, I took my bicycle and went to my fire station to make myself available for service, since damage could be seen all around. I did not get very far on bicycle, because the streets were hardly passable because of bomb craters, fallen masonry, and fallen trees. With great effort, I was finally successful in reaching my duty station, Firehouse 1. I took over the leadership of my brigade and departed with my Emergency Squad at 1:43 a.m. in the direction of Repsoldstrasse.'

An officer of the Civil Defence Police Ambulance Corps, Group I/III, described the events he was involved in during the raid of 24/25 July:

A rescue troop of five men of the Ambulance Corps 1/III pushed into the sea of flames at Schaarsteinweg to execute a rescue. The houses on this street were already in flames from roof to basement. Thick fire and smokescreens blocked the view and gave the impression of a complete wall of fire. Burning beams in the middle of the street strengthened the impression of a closed wall of fire. By going around single fires and jumping over fire sources in the street, the troop arrived at the rescue site; however, they were unable to effect the rescue. On the way back, it was ascertained that in the gaps between the flames there were at least 20 persons at various spots who, in the belief that they were completely enclosed, did not want to move either backwards or forwards. These people were in Schaarsteinweg for quite some time (about a half to one hour). All persons were still ambulatory although they had smoke injuries and burns. However, Schaarsteinweg was hardly suitable for a continuing stay in the middle of the flames. The troop was then able to persuade about 10 to 12 men to join them and get out of the sea of flames under the troop's direction. This group dissolved at the fire house in Admiralitässtrasse, where from the waterside absolute safety was assured.

Experience has shown that in fires of this size many people remain to die because of the picture they get from smoke, sparks, and ashes that they are confronted with a solid wall of fire and they are so overwhelmed that they do not even make an attempt to get out. They remain at the spot that is temporarily less endangered and eventually fall victim to the spreading fire. Search parties are often very successful and are able to lead many startled and confused persons out of the flames and to safety.

Chapter 4

Attack and Return

The first glimpse of the target came when the dark line of the estuary appeared on the radar screens of the lead aircraft. Soon the Pathfinders began their work. Using radar navigation, they released their first markers over the chosen aiming point in the heart of the city. These markers burst into clusters of bright red and green flares that floated down through the haze, burning steadily above the rooftops. Additional markers followed to reinforce the aiming point and correct for drift. The crews of the main force behind watched eagerly for these lights, which would guide their bomb sights in the absence of moonlight or clear visual references.

The initial target indicators were accurate, but as the attack developed, smoke and dust from the early explosions began to obscure the ground. Some of the later markers fell slightly wide, and a few aircraft inadvertently bombed secondary areas. Nevertheless the concentration of fire and blast over the central districts grew rapidly. High-explosive bombs tore open streets and buildings, rupturing gas mains and water pipes. Incendiaries followed in dense clusters, igniting roofs, timber yards, warehouses, and residential blocks. Within minutes the heart of the city was ablaze.

From their vantage points high above, the bomber crews watched a spectacle both awesome and terrible. Sheets of flame leapt upward through the smoke, flickering red and orange against the night sky. Columns of sparks rose thousands of feet into the air. Explosions from bursting fuel tanks and munitions stores sent rolling clouds of black smoke across the river. Even seasoned veterans who had taken part in the worst raids on the industrial heartland of Germany were astonished by the scale of destruction unfolding below. Some compared the scene to a volcano, others to a gigantic furnace consuming the earth.

Enemy defences fought back fiercely despite the confusion caused by the radar countermeasures. Heavy anti-aircraft guns ringed the city and opened fire as soon as the first bombers appeared. Shells burst among the attackers in continuous patterns of white and red flashes. Searchlights probed the sky, their beams sweeping restlessly through the darkness. Although the radar jamming made it difficult to track individual aircraft, the sheer volume of fire posed a constant danger. Pilots wove their heavy bombers through the flak as calmly as possible, maintaining the straight and level flight required for accurate bombing while trusting to luck and the skill of their gunners to deter night fighters.

The countermeasures continued to protect the main body of the force. Enemy controllers, their screens overwhelmed by the descending strips, struggled to direct fighters onto the bombers. Interceptions were sporadic and often uncoordinated. When a fighter did appear, vigilant gunners usually spotted it first, allowing the pilot to take evasive action. Several bombers exchanged bursts of fire with attackers but managed to escape without serious damage. Only a handful were actually destroyed over the target area, an astonishingly low loss rate considering the size of the force and the importance of the city.

The leading Pathfinders descended to their designated release heights and began the critical task of marking the target. From their bomb bays dropped the first brilliant indicators, bursting into clusters of coloured lights that pierced the thin veil of cloud. These flares burned fiercely as they drifted downward, their reflections glimmering off the river below and the rooftops of the sleeping city. Observers in the following waves of bombers used these glowing markers as their guide, adjusting their course and altitude to concentrate their loads on the designated aiming points. Within minutes the first heavy bombs were falling, their detonations sending towering columns of smoke and sparks into the night sky.

The initial explosions ripped through warehouses, shipyards, and residential blocks alike. Shockwaves rolled outward from each detonation, shattering windows and scattering debris across wide areas. Fires began almost immediately, fed by dry summer conditions and the tightly packed wooden structures of the city's older districts. Incendiaries followed the high explosives, cascading from hundreds of bomb bays in a relentless shower. Their magnesium cores ignited upon impact, each small fire combining with countless others until entire streets glowed red beneath the smoke. The thin clouds above reflected the flames, casting an eerie orange halo that was visible for miles and giving the bomber crews a clear view of their target.

Wave after wave of heavy bombers arrived over the city, each formation guided by the markers and by the growing inferno itself. The roar of engines, the whine of falling bombs, and the thunder of detonations merged into a continuous, deafening cacophony. Anti-aircraft guns fired desperately from the ground, their shells bursting amid the bombers in bright flashes of white and red, but the sheer number of attacking aircraft overwhelmed the defenders. Searchlights struggled to hold targets against the drifting smoke and the blinding glare of the fires. The radar deception continued to sow confusion, forcing enemy fighters to hunt blindly through a sky already crowded with the echoes of thousands of drifting strips.

Inside the bombers, the crews focused on their tasks with grim efficiency. Pilots held steady courses through the turbulence caused by the heat rising from the burning city. Bomb aimers released their loads with calculated precision, calling for minor adjustments in heading or altitude to achieve the best accuracy. Navigators recorded positions and times while wireless operators maintained a watch for any signals indicating a change of plan. Gunners scanned the fiery chaos below for signs of enemy fighters, occasionally firing short bursts at fleeting shadows in the smoke. Many crews were awed by the scale of the destruction they witnessed, but training and discipline kept them focused on survival and the completion of their mission.

The attack continued for nearly an hour as successive waves maintained the pressure. Each new arrival found the target area more clearly illuminated by the flames, allowing even greater accuracy despite the dense smoke. Some crews reported turbulence so violent that their heavy aircraft were tossed about like small boats in a storm, the updrafts from the firestorm lifting them hundreds of feet in seconds. Instruments wavered wildly and engines strained as pilots fought to maintain control. Yet the bomb runs continued, the stream of aircraft pouring a steady torrent of explosives and incendiaries onto the already devastated city.

Eventually the final markers signalled the end of the main attack. The last bombers released their loads and turned for the long journey back across the North Sea. Behind them the city burned with a ferocity that would continue for many hours, the combined heat of countless fires feeding the unstoppable firestorm. Columns of smoke rose miles into the air, lit from within by the glow of still-burning structures. The defenders, still confused by the continuing radar deception, struggled to organize a coherent pursuit as the attackers withdrew.

The bombers, having lost only two aircraft since leaving the target, turned from Germany and set course for the final leg across the North Sea to England. For all but one more crew, this homeward journey was as calm as they could have wished. Far out to sea, a German night fighter was patrolling near the Dutch Frisian island of Terschelling. Directed by ground control, the pilot closed in on a lone bomber that was moving unusually slowly, and on the first attempt he overshot it. Two engines on the same side were dead, leaving the aircraft limping toward England. The pilot hesitated, sensing that this damaged machine had already survived fierce action over Hamburg and had somehow made it so far.

For a moment he considered letting it continue, but duty prevailed and he pressed the attack. He aimed with care, striking at the wing tanks despite a reluctance to destroy the struggling crew. He later reported that he believed the bomber to be a Halifax, surprised that it carried no radar-jamming protection, and noted that it was well south of the main stream, probably taking a desperate shortcut. With no survivors and the wreck sinking into the sea, the aircraft could not be positively identified, but it was almost certainly a Lancaster of 103 Squadron, the third of that unit lost that night. All three of their fallen aircraft came to rest in the North Sea.

These losses were tragic, yet they stood out precisely because so many others escaped. The widespread use of radar-confusing foil allowed more than 700 bombers to pass safely through the German defences. By the time the first aircraft began landing in England, the night was still dark. The earliest to touch down arrived just after three in the morning. There were three landing accidents. One occurred when a Lancaster circling its home field to wait for clearance unexpectedly found another aircraft rushing head-on at terrifying speed. The navigator shouted a warning as the pilot forced his aircraft downward in a violent dive. Another Lancaster flashed overhead, close enough for its propeller to slice away part of the mid-upper gun turret and even shave a piece from the gunner's helmet, yet somehow both aircraft survived to land despite damage to two engines on the other machine. The experienced pilot of the first Lancaster would later go on to play a pivotal role as Master Bomber in a critical raid on a German V-weapon site, surviving the war despite this near miss.

Two Wellingtons of a Polish squadron also met trouble on landing. One, captained by a pilot making his very first flight in command, was forced to crash-land near the Lincolnshire coast after suffering difficulties on the return crossing. Though the aircraft was destroyed, the crew escaped without serious injury. Tragically, the young pilot would be killed on his second operation later in the same campaign.

The second Wellington found itself in a more comical predicament. Approaching what appeared to be a proper flarepath, the crew touched down smoothly, only to discover they had landed not at their airfield but on a decoy lighting site hidden in open farmland. The lights stood high on poles, glowing eerily above a field of tall corn. As the bewildered crew clambered out, they realized they were standing in stalks taller than their heads. Their confusion turned to laughter when a breathless airman arrived, apologizing for failing to fire the warning flare because he had been distracted by the attentions of a lonely widow in a nearby farmhouse.

The night's final landing came at a northern base just after five in the morning, exactly seven and a half hours after the first aircraft had taken off to open the massive raid on Hamburg. A Canadian pilot brought in his Halifax safely, marking the end of a remarkable operation. Only one bomber had been lost through a crash on return, and there were no crew fatalities in the landing mishaps. Aircrews, though stiff and weary, reported to their debriefings buoyed by the astonishing success of the radar-jamming measures. The mood was almost jubilant. Many spoke of the eerie but exhilarating sense of safety and the sudden belief that the balance of the air war might have shifted. They knew the advantage might not last, but morale soared nonetheless.

Of the 792 bombers dispatched, 732 struck the Hamburg area, with only twelve missing in action and one written off after a crash landing. Thirty-one others returned with damage. German night fighters, seventy-eight of them operating in five groups, had probably accounted for ten bombers, many of them stragglers or aircraft caught outside the main bomber stream. Only two bombers appeared to have been brought down in the heart of the stream itself. The defenders suffered at least two certain losses of their own. Anti-aircraft guns, thrown into confusion by the jamming, claimed only two victims. Among the British losses were four Lancasters from one group, four Halifaxes from another, three Stirlings from a third, and a single Wellington, while other groups escaped without a single loss. Strikingly, many of the lost crews were veterans, several with ten or more missions completed, a reminder that experience offered no guarantee of survival. Eighty airmen were killed and seven captured, including Jack Sowter.

Other Allied operations that night also achieved success without loss. Minelayers sowed explosives at the mouth of the River Elbe, specialist aircraft tracked enemy radar signals, Mosquitoes struck at northern German cities, and long-range bombers returning from North Africa dropped bombs on an Italian port en route home. Leaflet flights and supply drops to Resistance forces in France were likewise completed. The only German counteraction consisted of a handful of minelayers operating near the Humber. Thus ended the first night of the great assault on Hamburg, a night of devastating attack, narrow escapes, and a striking triumph for the new tactics that shielded so many aircrews from the deadly defences below.

For the crews who had taken part, the return to base brought a mixture of relief and exhaustion. Many had been in the air for more than seven hours, enduring intense cold, constant vibration, and the ever-present threat of sudden death. Ground personnel greeted them with hot drinks and brief words of congratulation before they were debriefed by intelligence officers eager for every detail of the operation. Pilots and navigators recounted their experiences of flak concentrations and fighter encounters, bomb aimers reported on the effectiveness of the target indicators, and wireless operators described the confused German radio traffic they had monitored. Mechanics swarmed over the weary aircraft, checking for damage and preparing them for the next mission. The raid marked a turning point in the air war. The successful use of radar-confusing foil demonstrated that the once-formidable night-fighter system could be neutralized, opening the way for further large-scale attacks on previously well-defended targets. In the devastated city, the fires burned for days and the suffering of the civilian population reached unprecedented levels. For those who had flown through the fiery skies, the memory of the great raid would remain vivid: the endless expanse of dark sea, the sudden blaze of target indicators, the towering columns of smoke and flame, and the knowledge that their efforts had unleashed destruction on a scale rarely witnessed in human history.

The night drew to a close with the last bombers landing at their scattered bases, engines ticking as they cooled in the cool early morning air. The crews, drained of adrenaline, made their way to brief rest before the cycle of preparation began again. Though many had narrowly escaped death, they knew the campaign was far from over. More raids would follow, each demanding the same courage, precision, and endurance. But for this night, the first great blow of the campaign had been struck, and the defenders had learned that their once-reliable system could be rendered powerless by new methods of attack. The balance of the night war had begun to shift.

Chapter 5

Did the Ends Justify the Means?

If measured by the level of destruction caused, Operation *Gomorrah* was arguably the most successful bombing operation of the entire European war, especially when measured against the Casablanca Directive's aim of bringing about the 'progressive destruction and dislocation of the German military, industrial and economic systems and the undermining of the morale of the German people to a point where their capacity for armed resistance is fatally weakened.' British and US Air Force commanders were instructed to use every opportunity 'to attack Germany by day to destroy objectives that are unsuitable for night attack, to sustain continuous pressure on German morale, to impose heavy losses on German day fighter force and to conserve German fighter force away from the Russian and Mediterranean theatres of war.'

Air Vice Marshal Harris' actions were further defined by an Air Staff directive, dated 14 February 1942, which stated: 'The ultimate aim of the attack on a town is to break the morale of the population which occupies it. To ensure this we must achieve two things; first, we must make the town physically uninhabitable and, secondly, we must make the people conscious of constant personal danger. The immediate aim, is therefore, twofold, namely, to produce (i) destruction, and (ii) the fear of death.'[5]

---

[5] John Grehan & Martin Mace, *Bomber Harris, Sir Arthur Harris' Despatch on War Operations 1942-1956* (Pen & Sword, Barnsley, 2014), p.23.

According to the United States Strategic Bombing Survey (USSBS), the death toll from the bombing and resultant firestorm was 42,600, with a 64% drop in Hamburg's population resulting from the 973,000 people that were assessed either to have been killed, evacuated or fled the city and its environs. This was achieved for the loss of only eighty-seven RAF aircraft, a relatively modest rate of attrition. If any Combined Bombing Offensive operation could illustrate the effect of strategic bombing on morale, Operation *Gomorrah* would surely be it.[6]

The level of destruction, due to the unexpected phenomenon of the fire storm, was unprecedented – though this was repeated at Dresden and Tokyo later in the war – resulted in a huge displacement of the population. Goebbels described it as the 'greatest migration of all time'.[7]

As early as 26 July, people were leaving the city in such large numbers, travel restrictions were imposed by the police:

Departure from Hamburg, until further notice, is allowed only with a special permit, with certain exceptions. A special permit is not required for (a) persons who, by passport, identification card, or census certification, can prove that they have no permanent residence in Hamburg; (b) members of the Army, Waffen-SS, police, Organization Todt, and federal Labour Service having either furlough papers or marching orders; (c) members of federal agencies or officials of the party if they can prove that their trip is in the line of duty; (d) persons with travel certificate issued by the social service or transportation

---

[6] Warren Huggins, 'Strategic Bombing and Morale: To what extent did Operation GOMORRAH affect British and German Morale?' *Air Power Review* vol.20, issue 3, p.53.

[7] D. Süss, *Death from the Skies* [*Tod aus der Luft*], trans. L. Sharp and J. Noakes (Oxford University Press, Oxford, 2011), p.77.

certificate issued by the party; and (e) foreigners with diplomatic passports.

Some indication of the widespread abandonment of the city can be gleaned from a notice which was distributed on 5 August:

All persons who are departing or have left Hamburg are urgently requested to report their present addresses immediately to the nearest police station, so that inquiries may be handled promptly.

Inquiries regarding the whereabouts of missing persons must be directed to Hamburg Census Office. All inquiries must contain the following, in plain writing or printed: Name, current address, Hamburg address of the inquirer, as well as name and personal data on the missing person.

As announced several times previously even those persons still in Hamburg who were registered as residing in Hamburg on July 25, 1943, and thereafter must report at once to the police precinct in the district in which they now reside. The report must be submitted on a form designed for this purpose, which is available at the police stations.

Buildings abandoned by those fleeing the bombing proved a temptation to some who looted empty properties. Those caught were executed.

In contrast to preventing people from leaving Hamburg, when some started to return, the problem of housing such returnees became so critical only essential workers were permitted entry:

WOMEN AND CHILDREN! STAY AWAY!
In the last few days, an increasing number of women and children have returned to Hamburg. This is neither advisable nor desirable. We now need men and unencumbered women of

working age in Hamburg. Those not in this category moving back to Hamburg may find that neither food nor lodging is available to them. And they should not expect public agencies to give them preferential treatment. Their premature return only means an unnecessary burden on food and transportation facilities, which should be employed for the sole benefit of the work forces now active in Hamburg.

A similar appeal was made on 9 August:

To ease the Hamburg traffic burden at the present time, travel into Hamburg is permitted only by those persons who have work to do in Hamburg.

Persons not able to produce proof to this effect will not be carried on any form of public transportation and they will not be permitted to leave from the railroad stations at Altona, Eidelstedt, Elbgaustrasse, Altrahlstedt, and Harburg. The police are empowered to close off any and all of these railroad stations if they consider it necessary. Those who travel to Hamburg without authority are in danger of finding neither food nor quarters.

The above restrictions are necessary in the Interest of the working population of Hamburg and to ensure the care and transportation of women and children emigrating from Hamburg.

All this had demonstrated, more than the previous bombing attacks, the devastation of Hamburg brought the German Home Front into the frontline every bit as much as on the battlefield. The Allies' willingness to decimate an entire city, and tens of thousands of its civilians, presaged not just their eventual victory but also the nuclear destruction of Hiroshima and Nagasaki. Nor did the Allies stop targeting Hamburg, whose war industry largely recovered within months.

Four attacks, each of more than 700 aircraft, were made by Bomber Command, and two small daylight attacks on the dock area by the USAAF. Well over 800 tons of bombs were dropped on the area, in spite of the failure of the last heavy night attack. This concentrated attack upon the bity became known in Hamburg as 'The Catastrophe', with some 40,000 people being killed.

Operation Gomorrah was planned and carried out as a single operation. Commencing on 24/25 July with a night raid, followed by American daylight attacks on the 25th and 26th, the climax was reached with the very effective night raids of 27/28 and 29/30 July. Space between attacks gave no time for the city to recover, so that the effect was one of continuous assault. This was augmented by Mosquito harassing attacks in the intervals. Large scale attacks were continued on Ruhr towns in the intervals, to prevent a concentration of defences at Hamburg.

The scale of attack upon the city was unprecedented. On the four night raids, a total of 3,095 aircraft were dispatched. A total of 8,622 tons of bombs were dropped, including 4,309 tons of incendiaries. The German police report gives the average number of bombs per square kilometre on the first raid as 7 landmines, 147 HE bombs, 17,580 stick incendiary and about 500 other incendiary bombs. On the second raid the density was about five times as great. Over 700 aircraft were employed on each attack.

The plan of attack on each of the big raids was similar. Route markers were dropped at a given point off the mouth of the Elbe, H2S aircraft marked the target, with a large force of backers-up to maintain the marking throughout the attack. Among these at intervals were crews expert in the use of H2S, whose duty was to recentre the attack when necessary. A total of seventy-four H2S aircraft were despatched. Backers-up were ordered to overshoot, usually by two seconds, the centre of the markers, so as to avoid the usual creep-back of the attack. Window was dropped by all aircraft while in the dropping zone at the rate of one bundle per minute from the maximum height possible. As mentioned, a few Mosquitos were despatched to other targets to create diversions.

On the first raid visual markers were employed, but their Target Indicators were scattered round the aiming point. As a result, the early attack developed four distinct concentrations. Later the attack was centred, but it began to creep back towards the end. 'By zero plus 30', it was noted, 'a long carpet of incendiaries extended back along the line of approach for seven miles.' Losses on this raid were abnormally low (1.5 per cent) due to the use of Window.

RT traffic overheard showed the confusion into which the fighter defences were thrown. One remark was 'It is impossible – too many hostiles.' The anti-aircraft guns were also affected, as evidenced by the minor flak damage experienced and the searchlights wandered aimlessly about the sky.

The final attack on 2/3 August was largely abortive owing to bad weather. Casualties were small, and many bombs fell in areas already devastated.

The annihilating effects of this series of raids can be shown by a few figures:

900,000 people homeless and missing 40,385 houses, and about 275,000 flats destroyed or badly damaged, as well, as 580 factories, 80 military, 22 transport and 2,632 commercial units; also 12 bridges and 180,000 tons of shipping sunk, of this was refloated later.

A Ministry of Home Security assessment was made in December 1943 as to the effects of these raids on German military capabilities. It estimated that about ten 500-ton submarines were lost, and about five Blohm and Voss aircraft.

There was a small loss of oil through storage fires, but the two refineries damaged were not essential, as excess capacity existed elsewhere. The ratio of industrial to non-industrial damage was assessed at 21 per cent to 79 per cent.

Port activity, at an average level of 200,000 gross tons before the raids dropped to 15,000 tons on 1 August, rising gradually to 75,000 tons on 18 August, 163,000 tons on 7 September. After this it dropped again to 75,000 on 9 October.

Post-war research throws light on the accuracy of these estimates. The output of 500-ton submarines was reduced by two or three per month. As the type was becoming obsolescent no real effort was made to improve on this figure.

The Blohm and Voss works were only being used for contract work for Messerschmitt aircraft of a low priority. The other aircraft factories had been evacuated. There was a production loss of oil of about 40 per cent for a month after the raids, mainly as a result of shortage of electricity. There was a temporary drop of about 30 per cent in port activity in August 1943.

After the war, Nazi minister for armaments and war production Albert Speer told interrogators that the firebombing of Hamburg 'made an extraordinary impression' on Hitler's closest advisors and that he'd advised Hitler similar Allied attacks 'might bring about a rapid end to the war.'

To the British public, the raid was justified in the kind of terms portrayed in the national press. Such an example is that of the *Daily Express*: 'It will be a long time before this is finished and a full count made of all the industrial damage. But it is already known that many important factories, in addition to those previously announced, have Great damage has been caused been hit and severely damaged. to the central and dock quarters, particularly in the Grasbrook, Billwärder Ausschlag and St Georg districts. So, it is clear, that each visit by the RAF is directed at knocking out great sections, making a full pattern that will leave no industrial part immune from the devastation.'

The American conscience was untroubled by the destruction, the Associated Press report of 6 August describing the RAF area bombing which struck residential districts as an integral part of the Allied offensive:

> Experience has shown that, in other area-bombed cities, the Germand have been able to repair their factories and move the bulk of the civilian population out. This latter, however, was done, not on humanitarian interest for the comfort and safety of the civilians, but merely as the quickest and cheapest way of providing new houses for the essential workers in the war industries. To prevent that, the wrecking of housing becomes necessary

The bomber crews themselves largely believed in what they were doing. The historian Martin Middlebrook quotes one unnamed pilot: 'I did, indeed, think about the types of target attacked but had few qualms, if any. But, having followed the march of the Nazis to war, cheered on by almost every German, and remembered the way in which they acted at Warsaw, Rotterdam, Belgrade, Coventry, London, etc., I could only feel that their turn was long overdue.'[8]

---

[8] Martin Middlebrook, *The Battle of Hamburg, The Firestorm Raid* (Penguin, London, 1988), p.348.

PART TWO

HEAD FIRST INTO THE NIGHT

Chapter 6

Preparation and Take-off

RAF Station Breighton, near Selby, in Yorkshire, was the home of 78 Squadron, 4 Group Bomber Command, and a satellite of 76 Squadron based at nearby Holme-on-Spalding Moor.

The Squadron was equipped with Handley Page Halifax mid-wing monoplane bomber aircraft with a wingspan of almost 100 feet, a length of 70 feet and stood almost 21 feet from the ground.

Although the Halifax was designed, originally, to take two Rolls Royce Vulture 2,000 h.p. in-line engines the specification was changed to four Rolls Royce Merlin 1,200 h.p. engines.

It is believed the reason for the change was due to the Vulture engine not being as successful as had been hoped whereas the Merlin engine was well established and fitted to both the Hurricane and Spitfire fighter aircraft.

Although the Vulture engine saw service in both the Avro Manchester bomber aircraft and the Hawker Tornado fighter aircraft, both types were phased out and replaced, respectively, by the Avro Lancaster bomber aircraft equipped with four Merlin engines and the Hawker Typhoon fighter aircraft equipped with the Rolls Royce Griffon engine.

Armament consisted of a four-gun Boulton and Paul power-operated turret in the tail, a two-gun mid-upper turret and a two-gun turret in the nose.

The all-up weight of 63,000 lbs. included a bomb load of 10,000 lbs. which was, usually, a combination of high explosives and incendiaries.

The Nissen hut in which we were billeted was sited to the south of the airfield and across the road from the River Derwent in which, occasionally, we splashed around. A visit, in 1993, snowed the hut still standing, albeit in a somewhat dilapidated condition and looking very forlorn.

Our crew was comprised of: Pilot Les Maidment from Maidenhead; the Bomb Aimer was Sergeant Les Croad from Cowes, Isle of Wight; our Wireless Operator was Sergeant Bill Robertson, a Yank in the RAF, from New Mexico and with a remarkable likeness to film star Victor Mature; the Mid-Upper Gunner was Sergeant J Bobby Roberts, from Oswestry; the Rear Gunner was Jock Ferguson from Glasgow; I was, of course, the Navigator.

We six crewed up at Operational Training Unit, Lossiemouth and were joined at Conversion Unit, Marston Moor by the seventh member, Flight Engineer Sergeant Joe Fagan, from Sheffield.

27 July 1943 dawned with clear skies and promised to be a continuation of the balmy summer days of that year.

As usual, after breakfast we went along to the Crew Room and found we were detailed, that evening, for Operations, but with a change of aircraft – JD 148. Our own aircraft was to be flown by the Crew detailed for Special Reconnaissance, i.e. to remain over the Target until the Stream of which we were part had completed bombing.

The Operation was split, usually, into six Streams with a time interval between each Stream and, dependent on the aircraft make-up, a different altitude. We flew at 20,000 ft.

On the way over to the aircraft dispersal area we chatted as to the possibility of the Target. My thoughts were that it had to be Hamburg, the reasoning that it was bombed on 24 July, should have been the Target on the 25th, but as reconnaissance showed that it was still obscured by smoke, we went to Essen instead. But as time would tell all would revealed at Briefing. Arriving at dispersal, it was evident why the change of aircraft – our own was new and JD 148 showed distinct signs of wear and tear.

We carried out the normal Daily Inspection and, as JD 148 was not our own aircraft, all items were double checked.

Mid-morning, after the NAAFI wagon had served tea and wads, sitting on the grass talking to the Ground Crew the reason for the change became even more evident as we were told the aircraft had been well, and truly, flogged and its maximum ceiling was 17,000 ft. The thought of being 3,000 ft below the remainder of the Stream was not at all endearing because at that height we could be a sitting duck and also we had heard the tales of aircraft being bombed by those above them.

After lunch my first chore was to collect navigation charts in readiness for the evening and then, once more, out to dispersal and a final inspection of the aircraft.

The afternoon passed quickly and without incident. Then it was back to the Mess for tea which was followed, firstly by Navigational Briefing and, secondly, by Crew Briefing.

Yes, it was to be Hamburg. The squadron was to be on maximum effort and, after two Crews had been publicly castigated for turning back on the previous raid, it was impressed upon us that the overall take-off time was to be improved. The space between aircraft, queueing for take-off, was to be reduced to the minimum and as soon as the preceding aircraft started to roll down the runway, the next in line was to immediately fill the vacant slot.

Between Briefing and Supper, my time was occupied in initial preparation of the Flight Plan and marking in the known Flak areas.

During supper I remarked that I had better collect my laundry, where-upon the Rear Gunner told me not to be such a damn fool, or words to that effect, as we might not come back. Whether that was premonition or a Scotsman's alleged tightness with money I do not know, sufficient for me to say that *my* laundry remained uncollected.

After supper, we had the meteorology report which enabled me to complete the Flight Plan. Then it was away to collect the Mae West, parachute and harness. Pockets were emptied of all means of identification and Mae West and harness were strapped on, making sure the latter was correctly adjusted.

Boots were changed for flying boots and with parachute in one hand and Navigation bag in the other I trundled outside to await transport to the aircraft. Once in the truck, I always looked out for a reply wave from the Padre.

We were dropped off, crew by crew, and we had a final check to ensure there were no tell-tale signs of Glycol leaks. There was time for a final cigarette and to relieve one's self. An Air Ministry Instruction had recently been issued forbidding the common practice of urinating over the tailplane. As we were about to clamber aboard, a truck came racing round as some crew member had forgotten his parachute. We were able to confirm that none of us was the culprit.

So the time had come, we were all aboard and occupying our take-off positions. The Bomb Aimer was in the Second Pilot's seat in order to assist with take-off, the Flight Engineer at his control panel and the Rear and Mid-upper Gunners, Wireless Operator and myself in the middle of the aircraft in what was commonly known as the Rest Position.

It was said that when a Halifax crash landed, it split into three sections and with the centre section being the strongest. Having witnessed two crash landings, that I can confirm.

The first occasion was at Marston Moor when we were detailed for three engine landings and for which we were augmented by a Staff Pilot.

Whilst at dispersal waiting to clamber aboard, an aircraft on a similar exercise was on the final approach with one engine feathered. Suddenly one of the remaining three engines failed. Obviously the Staff Pilot took over the controls and with the undercarriage partially retracted he neatly put it down in the next dispersal area. The aircraft broke into three sections - front, middle and rear. The crew scrambled out uninjured but visibly shaken.

However there was a funny side to this – the sight of one of the Ground Crew racing across the grass hotly pursued by one of the landing wheels. Needless to say, the Airman out-distanced the wheel.

The second occasion was on 22 July. We had not been detailed for Operations and were watching the Squadron take off. Halfway down the runway, an aircraft lost power and although the Pilot throttled back the engines the speed was too great for the brakes to take effect resulting in the aircraft over-shooting the end of the runway, careering over the grass and through the hedge onto the road which, fortunately, was devoid of traffic, through the second hedge and into the potato field. The aircraft slewed round in the soft ground, the under-carriage collapsed and the aircraft sank to the ground and broke into three sections – front, middle and rear.

The crew scrambled clear uninjured and, fortunately, neither the fuel tanks nor the bomb load exploded. Very quickly the fire crews were on site spraying the wreck with foam.

On the Halifax, the emergency exit procedure was for the Rear Gunner to rotate his turret so that it was at right angles to the fuselage, open the doors and fall out backwards. The Mid-upper Gunner and Flight Engineer would leave through the main entrance door, the Navigator, Wireless Operator and Bomb Aimer, in that order, through the hatch beneath the Navigator's seat and, finally, the Pilot would leave through the hatch above his head.

One by one the Merlin engines were started, run up to maximum revs and then throttled back to idling revs whilst we waited to move out of the dispersal area so that we would be in the correct pecking position for take-off.

Twenty-six aircraft sat waiting, patiently, for the green light – the first for take-off already on the runway and the remaining twenty five on the perimeter track.

On 23 July we had been in this same position when the Operation was aborted, but not so tonight. Up went the green very light, the leading aircraft revved up to maximum, the brakes were released and as it moved down the runway so the remaining aircraft moved forward one position until, finally, we were set to go.

We were given the green light and the throttles, with brakes on, were opened up to maximum. The brakes were released and we were away, gathering speed as we roared down the runway. We could feel the tail leave the ground and after one or two bumps the aircraft staggered into the air. The wheels were slowly retracted and finally locked in position.

Oh! the joys of hydraulically operated under-carriages. A far cry from the 145 turns of the handle, left handed, on the Avro Anson Mk. 1 at Air Navigation School.

The end of the runway disappeared beneath and we went into a slow left hand turn to start a circuit of the airfield. Time now for we four to take up our respective flying positions.

Chapter 7

The Final Flight of JD 148

Having settled myself in position, with parachute stowed beneath my seat, the contents of my Navigation bag transferred to the table and with Gee switched on, I gave the Pilot a course to Hexham. It had been established previously, by others, that a short cross-country flight was the easiest way to gain height and so avoid the maelstrom of aircraft climbing prior to starting the first leg of the Operation.

By the time we were due back at Breighton, we would be at the specified height and with only a short wait before setting course.

The forward crew positions were at a lower level than the main floor of the aircraft, with the Wireless Operator in front of the cockpit and the Navigator between him and the Bomb Aimer's position in the nose.

The outward flight was uneventful; three successive Gee fixes indicated a change of wind speed and direction which necessitated a slight course correction in order to comply with the Flight Plan.

The German coastline was crossed, on time, with nothing to report from either of the Gunners. At the specified time, the Mid-upper Gunner vacated his turret in order to start tossing out 'Window' through the flare chute. 'Window' were fine strips of metal, silver in colour and designed to blanket the enemy radar screens. It was first used on 24 July, resulting in a dramatic reduction in aircraft losses. However there appears to be a difference of opinion as to how long the success lasted. 'The Great Coup' is full of praise, but a report read at the Elvington Air Museum (home of 4 Group reunions) indicates that by 27 July, the Germans had found the answer.

This appears to be confirmed by research which appears to show the losses on the four Hamburg raids as twelve, twenty-two, thirty and thirty-five respectively.

The Bomb Aimer reported sighting the Target Markers ahead and took up his position in the nose. Run up to the Target was uneventful with the Bomb Aimer calling for slight course alterations. This gave me time to check the course for the first leg home.

Bomb doors were opened followed by the Bomb Aimer calling out the final course alterations, then it was 'steady, steady. steady, bombs away'. Simultaneously the automatic camera came into operation and I started counting, in reverse order, the required number of seconds during which time it was essential that level flight was maintained. It was very difficult not to subconsciously speed up the count towards zero, but temptation was resisted, zero was reached and I called out 'OK Skipper, take us home, course …'

As we turned on to course I switched off my light and drew back the curtain in order to have my customary quick look at the blaze down below and I always maintained that I preferred to see Blackpool Illuminations. Then with the curtain back in position and the light switched on it was back to work.

The first homeward leg was short in order to clear the Target Area and followed by a course alteration which would take us over the coast and to the safety of the North Sea.

It was not long after this course alteration that we were caught in the glare of searchlights but evasive action brought us into the clear. But as soon as we attempted to regain our course we were again picked up but more violent corkscrewing, by the Pilot, shook them off. Throwing a Halifax around the sky is not an easy matter and the Pilot was breathing heavily with the strain. It was a pity the Bomb Aimer was still in the nose otherwise he could have given assistance.

As soon as we regained course we were caught again, but this time it was by the dreaded radar controlled blue searchlight and immediately we were coned by others. No matter how the Pilot threw the aircraft around the lights followed and 'Window' did not appear to be having any effect.

The Bomb Aimer reported flak was coming up and immediately the Mid-upper Gunner called out that there was a hole in the fuselage between the flare chute and the tail, possibly caused by a shell passing through and failing to explode.

I felt a severe bump beneath the aircraft and immediately stood up and felt my backside, but there was no problem. I had heard the tale of a Navigator who always sat on his upturned steel helmet because he, in turn, knew a fellow Navigator who had received shrapnel wounds in his rear area.

I could see the altimeter and airspeed indicator falling, so it was no surprise when the call came from the Flight Engineer to 'feather the Starboard Inner' and quickly followed by 'feather the Port Outer'. Obviously, the bump I had felt was caused by two engines being hit by shrapnel.

So we had lost two engines and with that there appeared to be little chance of reaching home, merely a case of two options. The first would be to bale out over north-west Germany and the second the somewhat daunting prospect of coming down in the North Sea, even if successful not knowing if you would be picked up and if so by whom. Looking back there was the third alternative of baling out over the sea but that never entered my head.

Conjecture was not to last long as the order came to bail out. I folded my table and chair, retrieved my parachute and clipped it on to the harness, lifted the hatch cover and sat on the edge, facing forward, with my legs dangling in the slipstream.

At this point the Bomb Aimer was still in the nose and the Wireless Operator was standing behind me.

Taking a final gulp of oxygen, I removed my helmet and oxygen mask, put my head between my knees and dived, head first, into the night.

Whether or not I experienced a temporary black-out I am unaware, but I was brought to my senses by a jerk and looking upwards the parachute was billowing out. Certainly there was no recollection of counting the mandatory 'one, two, three' before pulling the rip-cord but this I must have done as the handle was still gripped firmly in my hand. Transferring the handle to inside my battle-dress blouse, I was able to use both hands to grip the harness straps.

Searchlights were still probing the sky but although looking all round there was no signs of an aircraft. I offered a silent prayer that I would not be caught by one of the lights as there were tales of that happening with the unfortunate victim being shot.

The parachute was swinging from side to side and attempts to correct the swing proved fruitless. What looked like either a layer of thin cloud or mist proved incorrect as I hit the ground with a bump and rolled over.

I lay there gathering my senses, fully convinced that it was all a bad dream and that I would wake up to find myself in bed. What wishful thinking. The reality was that I was in the middle of a field in north-west Germany, far from home and very much on my own.

As I did not feel any pain and there did not appear to be any signs of dampness or stickiness I decided that I was not injured and that was most definitely a plus.

I realised that I was still wearing my flying boots due, no doubt, to having a high instep and so although slipping down they had ledged half on and half off. It was later that I heard several tales of aircrew losing either one or both boots and having the painful experience of walking barefoot.

What was known as 'Escape' boots were only beginning to trickle through and although having been over to Holme-on-Spalding Moor, my size were out of stock.

Unlike the suede boots, the 'Escape' boots were in two parts, one part being a black lace up shoe to which was attached a zipped legging and which could be cut away so leaving the shoe. Even the necessary knife was included with the boots.

Each time I left home, after a leave, I always assured my Mother and my girlfriend that irrespective of where I went I would always come home even if it entailed walking back.

It was going to be a long walk home.

Strangely my Mother would never say 'Goodbye' but always 'Cheerio!'.

Chapter 8

Evasion and Capture

Silhouetted along the top of the field and also down the right hand side I could see houses and as there was not any sign of movement, it would appear that ·my descent and landing had not been observed. Yet another plus.

But a horrible thought struck me. As on my way down I had not seen any signs of an aircraft, had I imagined the 'bail out' call and were the others still on board and limping home?

Brushing the thought from my mind I stood up, removed my Mae West, gathered up the parachute and harness and walked towards the left side of the field. Fortunately the field was separated from the next one by a wide ditch with tall weeds which provided an admirable hiding place for my un-wanted clobber.

Turning left, I walked down the side of the field, through into a second field which, I was to find, led into a sandy track. The moon was just rising and, in the distance, could be heard the sound of the 'all clear'.

Suddenly I heard a cough and immediately froze. Peering through the hedge I could see the outline of a man standing in the open doorway of a house. He was bound to see me and that would be that. It did not occur to me that I could see him because the light was behind him and that there was no way he would be able to see me. After what seemed to be an interminable age but in reality was only a few minutes, he turned around, went indoors and closed the door behind him. I breathed a large sigh of relief.

The track eventually reached a road and as it wa a clear night it was possible to check my bearings from Polaris, or the North Star, and so I turned to the right and headed south.

Coming into a village and having crossed to the other side of the road, I had not walked many yards before I heard footsteps. I must admit I felt somewhat panic stricken. What should I do? Was my brief spell of freedom to be terminated? How far away were the footsteps? Deciding that it was not possible to hide, it was a case of being brazen and carry on walking.

The footsteps came nearer and my heart thumped louder, when out of the gloom appeared a woman and child, obviously on their way home after the 'all clear'. No other reason for them to be out in the wee small hours. They were bound to speak but no, they passed by without a murmur. Once again I breathed a sigh of relief and yet another once I was clear of the village.

Walking along the open road, hearing the sound of a car I raced across the road, climbed over a fence and lay flat.

Although the car passed by, I waited for it to disappear out of hearing before regaining the road and continuing my journey southwards.

It helped with being a moonlight night and reaching a crossroads there was sufficient light to read the signpost and see that I was heading in the direction of Oldenberg. Unlike back in England, the Germans had no thoughts of being invaded and so signposts had not been removed. With having vague recollections of its geographical position, I continued towards Oldenberg.

Dawn was breaking and hearing another car I scuttled down a steep bank on the right hand side of the road and waited.

The car came up to the crossroads and turned northwards and from whence I had come. Did that mean that they were looking for me or was it sheer coincidence? Whatever the reason there was no need for me to stay where I was, so it was back on my feet, climb up the bank and carry on walking.

As the day lightened, over to the right I could see a railway line but no sign of any trains. For a short distance, the road ran alongside a canal, or river, and the opportunity was taken to have a drink and also to fill the escape water bottle. This was made from rubber, balloon shaped, and one would expect it to expand when filled. But it did not and, when full, held about a cupful. Almost a dead loss but not quite as anything is better than nothing.

Continuing on my way, I thought I heard the sound of a bicycle and dived down the steep bank, on the right, and hid behind a tree. Although waiting several minutes, nothing passed by and so I decided that, possibly, I had heard a distant sound from the railway.

Regaining the road, I had not walked more than a hundred yards before I saw a soldier leaning up against his bicycle, quietly smoking his pipe and, horror of horrors, on my side of the road.

This had to be the end of my freedom. Never, ever was he going to let me pass him by and certainly not when he saw my battledress, no cap, suede flying boots and a water bottle hanging from my right hand. It might happen in films but not in the real world.

How wrong can you be? As I walked past he never uttered a word and you may be sure neither did I. Even out of the corner of my right eye I did not steal a glance. I held my breath as long as it was humanly possible and then some more. The temptation to quicken my pace was frightening, but I held on and continued at the same pace fully expecting to hear a shout, but the only sounds were those of my breathing and footsteps.

Corning up to a fork in the road, quite naturally I took the right hand and quickly reached a cluster of houses. From one of them, through a slightly open window, could be heard loud snores of someone deep in heavenly slumber.

Propped against the wall was a bicycle and it looked very tempting. On the premise that cycling is easier and quicker than walking and that all is fair in love and war, I decided that my need was greater than his.

So, I silently opened the garden gate, walked up the path – there was no need to creep wearing flying boots – and gently pulled the cycle upright.

To my relief there was not any noise, from the cycle, as I pushed it back up the path and then silently closed the gate behind me.

Once on the road I was quite content to push the cycle for the first fifty yards, or so, before mounting and pedaling away. The thought of his consternation, and possible outrage, when he discovered his pride and joy was missing never entered my head. Someone approaching and then the decision would be made for me. I did not have to wait very long and I veered over to the right.

Although I passed several early morning workmen, they in their wisdom chose not to make any form of greeting and if that was their attitude who was I to disagree and so I just ignored them.

After the next crossroads, I passed the morning milk – two girls pulling a hand trolley loaded with a couple of churns. What could I not have done to a pint but I had to resist temptation.

As more and more workmen began to appear I decided the time had come to look for cover and eventually spotted a small wood, or copse, over to the right.

Fortunately at this time, the road was deserted and as there was a track which ran alongside the southern edge I turned off the road. After some 200 yards I dismounted and pushed the cycle into the wood until I found some undergrowth where it could be hidden. Luckily I found another patch of undergrowth, about 50 yards away, into which I burrowed and very quickly was sound asleep.

I awoke at midday feeling hot, thirsty and rather grubby.

The sun was beating down with not a cloud to be seen and it looked as though the hot summer days were going to continue.

After slowly gathering my senses I decided to have a quiet look around, but as soon as I attempted to stand up there was a shooting pain in my right ankle. Sitting down and removing my boot and sock I found my ankle swollen but feeling all round it I decided that nothing was broken and that it was severely sprained. Obviously this had occurred when I hit the ground with my boots only half on. Also, with walking immediately and then cycling any pain had been deadened.

Eventually I managed to stand up, supporting my weight by holding on to a tree branch. Gently putting my weight on to it and then walking, or rather hobbling, a few yards I decided the pain was bearable. It had to be otherwise I could be stuck in the wood for quite some time. After a number of plusses this was a minus that I could have well done without.

So what were my assets? An empty water bottle and no idea where or when it could be refilled, an escape kit containing some Horlicks tablets, a tube of condensed milk, maps in the form of handkerchiefs, Occupied Country currency, a hacksaw blade about 2 inches long, two compasses – one made up of two buttons on my battledress blouse and the other a small flat bar hidden beneath the leather name tag above the right breast pocket, a few cigarettes, pipe, tobacco contained in a pouch which concealed an escape map, matches and the cycle. Plus what I suppose was the greatest asset – the fact that no one knew where I was.

Consulting the maps, I decided that it would be necessary to circumnavigate Oldenberg, preferably on the eastern side, and then to make a bee-line for Holland. My only worry was if the sprained ankle would stand up to the travelling involved.

Supreme optimist that I was, the thought of being captured did not even enter my head. Here was I, alive and well, and by now my Mother would have received the telegram saying that I was missing and there was no way that I could tell her not to worry. Although each aircraft carried a homing pigeon, when you are told to jump you jump and the last thing you would possibly think about would be the pigeon. Anyway, even if I had brought him with me you cannot write a message without pen and paper, neither of which did I have.

The other thought that crossed my mind was the flying rations which were still in my navigation bag. I must confess that although always drinking the orange juice, the chocolate was saved and given to one of the station WAAFs.

Having checked the cycle was still in its hiding place, the thought struck me that if it had not have been then I, too, would have been discovered.

Standing looking towards the edge of the wood I watched a man and woman cycling along the track. I was fairly well screened but they were more intent in talking to each other and looking where they were going than to glance in my direction.

Allowing more than sufficient time for them to disappear I limped to the edge of the wood and had a good look around. In the first field there was a stream winding its way along and with a path on the near side. In the distance there was a railway line but as a train did not pass by it was not possible to determine whether it was a main line or a country branch line.

As there was no sign of any activity I decided to take advantage of the stream to quench my thirst, re-fill the water bottle and, equally importantly, to bathe my ankle.

Feeling refreshed, I decided to take a walk along the path and in so doing almost came to grief.

In the next field to the left of the path, a woman was busily engaged in milking a cow but was so intent in what she was doing she did not give me a second glance, even if she had given me a first. Then to my great consternation there was a workman cleaning out the stream. To have turned around and retraced would have looked extremely suspicious so it was Robson's choice and hope for the best.

It is said that the Almighty looks down upon the righteous and also the Devil looks after his own. Either way I was fortunate that he chose to ignore me. Who knows, he may have thought it not unusual for someone in uniform and flying boots to be taking a stroll across the fields.

Just before reaching the railway line a dilapidated old train passed by hauled by a locomotive which would have not been out of place in a Hollywood Western or Emmett's Oyster Creek Railway. Smoke was belching out of a mushroom shaped smoke stack, the bell was clanging and there was even a cow-catcher on the front end. My earlier query was answered; it had to be a branch line.

Having crossed the railway line, the ground rose gently ending, at the far side of the field, with a shelf up to the next field and with a large shady tree to the fore.

Limping across the field, I settled myself down in the shade, closed my eyes and promptly fell asleep. I was awakened by the sound of loud voices and peering over the top of the shelf I could see a group of workers hay-making. Realising that this was not the place for me, as soon as they had worked back to the far side of the field I limped away.

Retracing my steps to my hiding place, although the milkmaid had finished and disappeared, the workman was still cleaning out the stream. However, as previously, Lady Luck was on my side, he chose to ignore me and soon I was safe and sound.

What I did not know until much later was that the milkmaid, hay-makers and workman were probably not German, but foreign labour and possibly either Polish or Russian. Although *we* had been given escape lectures such possibilities were not mentioned but, on the other hand, the lecturers did not have any first hand knowledge and it was more that likely the lectures were merely a morale booster.

Waiting is the worst part of evasion and even more so when you are on your own. Time passes so slowly and with nothing to do but sit and wait, time appears to pass even more slowly. It was worsened by being the end of July and obviously the days were much longer.

However, evening came and about 7.30 pm I decided to make a move. Hindsight showed that I should have waited until it was dark but another three hours, or so, seemed interminable.

My ankle, if anything, was worse and made walking extremely painful, but once back in the saddle it was easier and the pain gradually eased and virtually disappeared.

Thirst was also a problem as my water bottle was empty. It was not helped by the sight of numerous roadside signs extolling thirst quenching Coca-Cola or the local beer. If the advertisements had been for food that would not have worried me one little bit as the thoughts of food had not entered my head. That was to come in the future.

Although I cycled through several hamlets and small villages no-one showed the slightest interest. Even the policemen and also men in brown, or mustard, uniform and each carrying a pistol did not give me a second glance even though I was in RAF battledress, flying boots and without a cap.

Even an officer, in the rear seat of an open car, merely stared and, quite naturally, I stared back, strongly resisting the temptation to give him a wave.

Cycling past a roadside pool, with children splashing around, did not do my thirst much good either. So far, so good. The shadows were lengthening and soon it would be dusk and the darkness of the night.

I passed a sailor cycling in the opposite direction but he was not impressed. Then out of the corner of my right eye I caught a glimpse of two youths cycling on the pavement and appearing to keep pace with me. As I varied my speed, they did likewise but I was not unduly worried as the further I got from the village the less likelihood of them following me.

Then out of the corner of my left eye I could see the sailor who, obviously, had turned around, no doubt having been alerted by the wretched youths.

Although blandly cycling on, he caught up with me, pointed to my boots and shouted 'Flieger!' Choosing to ignore him, he forced me to stop and in my best schoolboy French explained that I was not a 'Flieger', and that I was going to Oldenberg.

We argued for about twenty minutes, he insisting that I was a Flieger and with me being equally adamant that I was not and that I was going to Oldenberg. The question of nationality did not arise.

Unfortunately, a soldier who spoke English appeared on the scene and the bluff became a losing battle. Eventually I gave up, admitted I was English and shook hands with the soldier.

My freedom was over and my impatience had received its just reward.

Chapter 9

Arrival at Obereussel

With the soldier on one side, the sailor on the other and the two youths bringing up the rear, I was escorted back to the last village. As we cycled along the soldier asked if I was wounded, but not considering that a sprained ankle constituted a wound, I assured him that I was unhurt. We chatted generally without touching on the subject of war and I suppose it could be said that he was quite friendly.

We stopped outside a house, on the right hand side of the road, and having parked the cycle, when I started to limp the soldier showed his concern and insisted that I must have been wounded. Again I assured him that, most definitely, I was not wounded.

Once inside the house I was handed over to two men, both in uniform, who spoke a little English. Apparently one of them was a doctor and as the soldier appeared to have voiced his concern he examined my ankle and confirmed that it was not fractured but had suffered a severe sprain. After he had applied a cold compress and bandages and I had pulled on my sock and flying boot I expressed my gratitude.

I was not searched but merely asked if I was carrying a pistol to which I was able to answer in the negative.

Having asked if it were possible to have a glass of water, I was shown into the adjoining room where there was a third man, in civilian clothes, and two rather good looking girls.

Whilst waiting for the glass of water, the civilian remarked on the niceness of the two girls and did I agree. Quickly biting the tip of my tongue, I diplomatically agreed instead of saying that I had seen better.

The glass of water was not forthcoming but instead I was given a pot of coffee. I say coffee but obviously it was ersatz and tasted of burnt acorns. Even though it was served black and unsweetened, my thirst was such that anything, virtually, would have been palatable.

I offered the civilian a cigarette and when he refused, asked if I may smoke but the request was not granted. However, when later a second civilian entered the room to enquire if I was comfortable, I replied in the affirmative but added that it would be nice to be able to have a cigarette. To my delight, the 'no smoking' rule was reversed.

Having finished the cigarette and still not having been searched I decided the time had come to take steps to ensure that as and when I was searched, nothing of importance should be found.

As concealment could not be accomplished in front of the present company I made a request to visit the lavatory. As none of us spoke the other's language, this was easier said than done, but eventually with the aid of sign language the penny dropped and I was escorted upstairs.

Fortunately my escort remained outside and I was allowed to close and lock the door. Sitting on the toilet seat I quickly removed my right boot and sock, unwound the bandage and removed the compress, the latter being deposited down the pan.

Having wrapped the escape handkerchiefs round my ankle and at the same time tucking the saw blade within the folds, on the underside of my foot, and inter-leaving the Allied currency as I re-bandaged my ankle. When the task was completed I surveyed my handiwork and decided that it was good enough to pass a cursory examination. Fortunately, it was not too bulky to prevent my pulling on my sock and boot after which I flushed the toilet ensuring that the compress had disappeared, washed my hands, unlocked the door and rejoined my escort. No doubt he thought that the smile on my face was one of relief and not one of satisfaction.

Having rejoined the ladies it was a case of waiting, in silence, until an officer appeared and after much heel clicking and Heil Hitler-ing I was handed over into his custody.

As I was ushered out or the room and as it is not possible to heel click in suede flying boots, I came to attention, bowed to the two girls and limped through the door.

Outside was an open, two-door, four-seater car and I was ordered to sit in the back. To my surprise the officer sat in front with the driver and, with not having been searched, if I had been carrying any kind of weapon it would have so easy to have over-powered them. But as was not armed all I could do was to sit and gaze at the countryside.

After arriving at an Army barracks, at Oldenberg, I was put into a cell and searched. Fortunately, the bandaged ankle was not disturbed due to my having the presence of mind to point out that my ankle had been examined by a German doctor and that it was he who had applied the bandages.

With wearing cuff-links my shirt sleeve covered *my* watch which escaped detection and, although my clothing was subjected to a fine tooth-comb search, the compasses were not discovered.

Having been ordered to get dressed, it was only my flying boots that were confiscated.

The cell door was left open which allowed the freedom to visit the toilet and bathroom but the door at the end of the corridor was locked.

Not knowing how long I might be in residence I decided to keep myself occupied and once all was quiet, retrieved the saw blade and began, laboriously, to saw through one of the window bars. With a saw blade a mere two inches in length it is a slow and difficult process and even more so with not having a handle.

In an attempt to prevent my fingers being cut I wrapped my hand in my handkerchief, which slowed down the operation due to it continually getting caught in the blade.

At the end of the night I was only part way through the bar and it was obvious that I would need to be here for several days, and nights, if there was to be any impact. Even then I had no idea what lay on the outside and any escape would be minus boots.

The following morning my boots were returned and I was escorted to an office where I was interrogated by a female civilian. Having given the regulatory Name, Rank, Number and next of kin, when asked where I was shot down I replied that it was not permitted to divulge such information.

When asked about the whereabouts of my comrades I replied that I did not have any and although the question was repeated I stuck to my story. At the end of question time I had the feeling that she was beginning to believe that the RAF were using single seat bombers over Germany.

On returning to my cell and having requested some food I was given some cold cooked meat, heavily laced with garlic, and dry black bread. If there had been something with which to wash it down it might have helped, but as there was not the bread was uneaten and I had only a little of the meat.

At lunch time I was given a large bowl of vegetable soup, some of which again I ate but the taste of garlic became too much. Everything appeared to taste the same and the same odour seemed to pervade the atmosphere.

During the afternoon I was escorted by an armed guard to the railway station so my efforts of the previous night had been in vain.

Whilst on the train, by using a combination of time and the position of the sun it was possible to determine the general direction of travel. Not that it mattered as the journey was short and it was not possible to establish the name of the station as the name board was in Gothic letters.

I was marched, or rather the guard marched whilst I limped alongside, to an airfield and handed over to the Luftwaffe.

Again there was no attempt to search, no doubt assuming that this had been effected previously, and I was put into a room occupied by two other aircrew, one of them being a New Zealand Air Gunner.

The room was furnished with chairs, table and double tier bunks and, surprise, surprise, the window was not barred. Not that it mattered as, rather unsportingly, the absence of bars was compensated by a guard armed with a machine pistol.

With an open window, thoughts began to formulate as to the possibility of, during the night and with the co-operation of the other two, overpowering him. With three against one, even though the guard was unarmed, and especially if one came from the rear, the odds did not appear to be completely on the side of the guard.

However the possibilities faded as, during the evening, we were taken back to the railway station. This time there were two guards, each carrying an automatic pistol, who made it quite clear that talking was strictly forbidden.

Once on the train it was a case of just sitting there and staring out of the window until the train reached out destination and we were ordered out on to the platform.

Obviously there was to be a delay before our next train as we were dumped, unceremoniously, in a basement room which was occupied by two prisoners, one a Frenchman and the other a Yugoslavian. With difficulty it was possible to talk to the Frenchman and bring him up to date with the latest war news and the help being given by the Resistance. The Yugoslavian produced some American tobacco and proceeded to hand-roll cigarettes in newspaper. Although it is said that fish and chips taste better in newspaper, the same does not, most certainly, apply to cigarettes. But as my cigarette supply was exhausted, they were better than nothing.

The guards returned and we three were taken up on to one of the platforms to await our connection. Although the sirens sounded an air raid warning and people started taking cover, I was not worried unduly as it had to be another raid on Hamburg. Luckily the civilians were not aware that we were members of the RAF otherwise they might have turned nasty.

As we waited a freight train steamed slowly through on the other side of the island platform but although there were a number of box-cars with the doors open my ankle prevented my making a spirited dash for freedom.

Our train pulled into the platform and we were ushered into a reserved compartment. Fortunately I managed to get a window seat, facing forward, opposite to the door into the corridor. The seats were wooden and as the night wore on they became more and more uncomfortable.

During the night whilst the train was moving slowly I requested permission to visit the toilet. Naturally I was accompanied but apart from relieving myself the main purpose of visiting the toilet was wasted as the window was non-opening.

In spite of being uncomfortable I did manage to dog sleep and during one spell of consciousness noticed there was a canal alongside the railway line.

As dawn broke revealing an early morning mist, we steamed through Giessen and I would estimate that our speed was no more than 20 mph. As the guards appeared to be asleep I carefully and noiselessly lowered the window. The guards still appeared to be asleep so I reached up to get one of the briefcases from the rack but, in so doing, I noticed that both guards had their pistols in their hands so, with discretion being the better part of valour I abandoned any idea of throwing the briefcase at them and, in the confusion, diving through the open window.

Eventually we arrived at Frankfurt-on-Main where we changed to a local train to Obereussel just a few miles distant. Here we boarded a tramcar and although one of the civilians sitting immediately behind me asked if I spoke French, apart from replying 'a little' that was the end of the conversation as the guard made it quite clear that talking was strictly forbidden. The word '*verboten*' was to become very much part of everyday life but as time passed there would be others which would form the basis of our limited vocabulary.

From the tramcar I limped towards a small encampment surrounded by barbed wire fences and which was to be 'home' for the next few weeks.

Chapter 10

Interrogation

I was taken to a small office and ordered to remove all my clothing. Whilst it was being searched quite systematically I drew attention to my bandaged ankle and that it had been examined, and dressed, by a German doctor. Although being informed that was neither here nor there and that it had to be removed, I ignored the instruction. By the time he had completed searching my clothing and had ensured there was nothing concealed in my mouth, up my nose, ears and rectum he had forgotten all about the bandaged ankle and ordered me to get dressed. This was one order I did not ignore and pulled on my clothes as quickly as possible.

Search over, I was escorted along the corridor and put into a room with two others who turned out to be aircrew of the American Army Air Force and who greeted me with great suspicion.

The room was about 10 feet square, furnished with one single bed which had been commandeered by one of them, the other enjoying the comfort of the floor. There was one window which was not barred but overlooked a 10-foot-high double barbed wire fence with coiled barbed wire in between.

Having asked the Americans if it were possible to get out and being told they had no idea, for starters I had a look at the door lock and by using the bar magnet as a screw driver I managed to remove it and gently open the door. A fractional opening was sufficient to see a guard complete with rifle and fixed bayonet positioned in the corridor. The door was reclosed quicker than it had been opened and the lock replaced. From then on I was accepted by the Americans.

Grub up, or chow as it was called by the Americans, at mid-day, or thereabouts, consisted of a bowl of soup, two slices of dry black bread and a small square of cooked meat washed down by a mug of mint tea, minus milk and sugar. In the evening and again at breakfast we had a further two slices of dry black bread washed down with a mug of black unsweetened ersatz coffee.

With the bed being occupied, I joined the other American in the comfort of the floor. At least you could rest your back against the wall of the hut but after a while it was a pleasure to get on your feet and pace the room.

Each evening our boots were taken away which appeared somewhat pointless as, at night, the perimeter fence was flood-lit and patrolled.

Although we were allowed to use the washroom, the morning wash was a cold sluice as soap was not provided and shirt tails had to double as towels.

During the second morning we were joined by another American, this time a pilot, who had attempted to bail out at 30,000ft but his leg became trapped. He estimated that he was down to around 2,000ft before succeeding in extricating himself and then Murphy's Law decreed that his parachute did not fully open. Fortunately, his fall was broken by the branches of a tree and he was lucky to survive with only a broken ankle. With his ankle in plaster he took pride of place on the bed.

Later we were joined by another American, an Air Gunner, who was sporting a black eye and several pieces of sticking plaster on his face. When asked the obvious question he replied that he was not injured but did concede that his face hurt.

One of his fellow Americans asked him which mission he was on when shot down. His reply was to the effect that he did not know the name of the target, but it was a daylight mission and they had flown over water. In point of fact he did not even know the day, or the date, of the mission.

We were joined by the Waist Gunner from a B29 Super Fort who was very bitter as when ordered to bail out, he chickened out and was pushed by another crew member. The fact that his fellow crew member had saved his life just did not seem to occur to him.

Yet another American joined the happy throng bringing our numbers up to six and the place was beginning to feel somewhat crowded. He was a Pilot, from Texas, and as mad as the proverbial Hatter. Having a lighter but no cigarettes or tobacco, he improvised by rolling straw from the mattress in newspaper and attempting to smoke the result. Just about all he did succeed in doing was to singe his eyebrows when his 'cigarette' went up in flames.

One morning an American, who had lost an arm, came round asking if anyone knew an RAF Bomb Aimer named Les Croad. Without hesitation I said 'Yes' and he told me that he was with him in Wilhelmshaven hospital where he had died after suffering severe internal injuries in addition to broken limbs. At the time it did not occur to me to ask the American his name and the consequence of this lapse did not become apparent until after I was de-briefed back in England.

So passed five days of physical discomfort made durable by the conversations with the Americans before being taken down to solitary confinement.

At least my cell was comparatively spacious and furnished with a single bed (no bedding apart from the mattress) and a chair. Surprisingly there was a large window, albeit barred, with a deep sill sufficiently large enough in which to sit in a slightly drawn-up knees position.

After the usual midday soup I lay, quite luxuriously, on the bed and dozed off, being awakened when an Officer, wearing a Red Cross armband, entered. I stood up and apologized for being asleep and, disarmingly, the Officer said not to worry.

He handed me a form, and pen, with a request that it should be completed. Having been forewarned of such forms, after divulging my name, rank, service number and next of kin, I read the remainder of the questions and then returned the form with the remaining spaces left blank.

After a cursory look he handed the form back to me with the request that I answer the remaining questions. I pointed out to him that as he was wearing a Red Cross armband he should be aware that under the terms of the Geneva Convention, to which both Germany and Great Britain were signatories, I was not required to volunteer any information other than that already given.

He changed the subject, asking if I enjoyed reading, to which I replied in the affirmative and that if a book, in English, were available it would be appreciated as it would help to pass the time.

Saying that he would make the necessary enquiries and after handing me a cigarette and allowing me to light up, he departed.

It was not long before he returned and minus any book. He insisted that the form should be completed but again I did not accede to his request and when faced with persistence calmly suggested that if the information he required was so vitally necessary he should contact the Air Ministry in London.

I am afraid that rendered him speechless and he turned on his heel and stormed out of the cell. No doubt the prospect of some reading matter was the proverbial carrot and that would be the end of that.

The following morning, with the help of sign language, I asked the guard if I might have a broom so that I could sweep out the cell. This was forthcoming and possibly appreciating the request, the guard intimated that if there were any 'left-overs' from the mid-day meal he would bring them to me.

Asking for a book was a little more difficult, but eventually he understood and said that he would ask the officer. As he would not, or could not, take me to the officer I suggested he should visit me.

I did not get an officer, but instead an English speaking civilian. Having explained about the book he said that he would approach the Kommandant. Obviously he was as good as his word as, during the afternoon, the guard brought in a selection of books from which I chose one by John Buchan.

Whilst in my usual position, in the window sill, some foreign prisoners walked past the window, but requests for a cigarette were to no avail. If this were solitary confinement then with being able to see the outside world go by it was not too much of a hardship.

Whoever was in the next cell attempted to start a conversation but it was soon curtailed by the guard who said, quite plainly, that talking was forbidden. Once again '*verboten*'.

The following day interrogation started in earnest, being taken to an office. After being given a cigarette and after confirming the details given on the 'Red Cross' form I was asked the number of my Squadron and its location and replied that I was unable to divulge that information. He talked generally and then asked the type of aircraft in which I was flying. Again I said that I was not allowed to divulge the information.

The interview ended and I was returned to my cell. So far so good.

The second day, in addition to again asking the previous day's questions, he asked the number of aircraft in the Squadron to which I replied that it was not possible to reply as the necessary information was not in my possession.

He asked what I was doing in civilian life before joining the RAF and not seeing any harm in answering the question replied that I was an Electrical Switchgear Drawing Office Apprentice.

The third day, after initially repeating the questions of the previous days, he handed me the Flight Plan retrieved from another aircraft and asked the meaning of the additional times shown on the first page. Having replied that the times, to me, were meaningless he insisted that as a Navigator I should know their meaning. This time I replied that quite often I would put various hieroglyphics on the Flight Plan as a reminder to carry out certain actions and that to a third person they would be completely meaningless.

He switched tactics and asked if I had any hobbies or interests to which I replied that I had always been interested in aircraft. To a further question I replied that such an interest could not be construed as warlike and that it was the evolution of aircraft that was my particular interest.

After further questions I intimated that if one looked at a particular aircraft manufacturer it was sometimes possible to trace the evolution and, as an example, said that you could see the sleek lines of the Supermarine Schneider Trophy seaplanes continue into the Supermarine Spitfire. Also that there was a similarity between the de Havilland Comet which flew in the pre-war London to Melbourne air race and the de Havilland Mosquito. I finalised by suggesting that no doubt he would find similar instances within the German aircraft industry.

On the fourth day, the heat was turned up in as much that he dispensed with any of the pleasantries. After the usual opening questions he went straight in and asked where I was shot down and the whereabouts of the remainder of my crew.

This brought my standard response of not having the relevant information.

Out of the blue he asked 'where was this place called 'Breighton' but as a German would he pronounced it 'Brighton'. Quite truthfully I replied that I had never been there and, untruthfully, added that before the war whilst going on holiday had passed through on route to a South Coast holiday resort.

This explanation obviously displeased him as he raised his voice and started to rant and rave. When I did manage to break in I suggested that if he required any further information could he not try the Air Ministry in London?

On the fifth day he became even more blunt and threatening. He brought up the question of my not having any means of identification which was correct as I was not wearing dog tags — all other forms of identification had to be left in your locker prior to take-off. Obviously there was no option but to agree, but when he said that lack of identification could provide sufficient justification for handing me over to the Gestapo and that I could be shot as a spy, I refused to be intimidated. Drawing myself to my rather inadequate five feet nine inches, I replied that an Englishman and a Gentleman did not indulge in untruths and that he should know, also, that the word of an Englishman was his bond.

Eventually he looked across the table and calmly informed me that I was Sgt. Jack Sowter, the Squadron was No. 78, I had been shot down on the night of 27 July and then proceeded to give the names, and ranks, of the remaining Crew members. Feeling rather deflated and crestfallen there was no option but to agree.

No doubt in an attempt to turn the screw he told me how many aircraft had been shot down the same night and when I replied that his claim appeared to be somewhat extravagant he immediately asked why his figure should not be accepted. Realising that he could be alluding to the effectiveness of 'Window' I countered by asking how many had been accounted for on the night of 24 July. Taking a leaf out of some of my responses he said that, unfortunately, he was not in possession of the relevant information. So ended the session and after being offered a final cigarette I was returned to my cell.

The following morning I was escorted down to the main camp, solitary confinement and interrogation were both behind me and the only regret was that there had been insufficient time to finish reading the book. But, that is life.

Chapter 11

Dulag Luft

The Camp consisted of a single compound surrounded by the usual double lane of barbed wire fencing and housed three wooden huts – Officers, Other Ranks and the Cookhouse/Messroom.

After being 'booked in' and given a tin of fifty Craven 'A' cigarettes I was shown my allotted room. After dumping my belongings, such as they were, on one of the vacant bunks I took advantage of the freedom to visit the other rooms in the hope there may be someone that I knew.

The first two rooms resulted in drawing blanks, but in the third were three of the other Crew members – Joe Fagan, Jock Ferguson and Bobby Roberts.

Joe told me that they had landed close to each other and in close proximity to the aircraft, to which they had been taken. At the scene they were told that the Pilot – Les Maidment – and the Wireless Operator – Bill Robertson – were still in the aircraft and both had been killed. In turn I was able to fill them in regarding the fate of Les Croad.

To what sort of interrogation they had been subjected I do not know as that was not discussed but it may have been superficial only and that due to the numbers involved with both RAF and USAAF prisoners, in depth interrogation may have been reserved for Pilots and Navigators only.

The first meal was something of an eye opener as it included tinned salmon. So this was how PoWs fared and were all the stories of the starving Germans mere figments of the imagination of the Ministry of Propaganda? Little was it realized that the meal was due to the contents of Red Cross food parcels, which at Dulag Luft were used communally as opposed to being issued individually. As a matter of fact, at this stage of being a PoW no one had even mentioned food parcels, let alone them being the basis for a food supply for an escape attempt.

As the Camp had a small library I took the opportunity to browse through the selection of books and came across *Hoyle's Compendium of Games* which included a section on Chess. With being able, also, to borrow a Chess board and Chess Men it was possible to play through various games, as the result of which, I decided to concentrate on Max Lang's Attack. After repeatedly playing though the opening moves it was possible to commit them to memory.

Brimming over with confidence I challenged Bobby Roberts to a game and to my complete surprise, and satisfaction, for the first time he was check mated.

At our level of play, Pawn to King four was the standard opening and so it was possible to use the opening moves for either attack or defence.

Letter forms were issued and it was possible to assure my Mother that I was safe and well. Additionally I included a request that if it should be possible the contents of my wallet should be given, as a small token of gratitude, to the WAAF who had packed the parachute that had saved my life.

Personal effects were returned but the tobacco pouch, watch (RAF issue), Horlicks tablets, small change and parachute handle were confiscated. Pleas that the handle was a souvenir fell onto deaf ears.

Through the auspices of the Red Cross Organisation we were kitted out with RAF issue shirt, socks, under-clothes, boots and great-coat. It was a joy to put on clean clothes and to wash through soiled items of clothing.

With nothing to do between meals, and certainly nowhere to go, the time between meals was spent either chin-wagging, reading or, in *my* case, playing Chess.

Although there were thoughts with regard to the possibility of an escape attempt, these were discounted due to the fact that the outside of the perimeter fence was constantly patrolled and at night was flood-lit.

The possibility of digging a tunnel was out of the question due to the lack of tools and a suitable starting point. Also, there was the question of the disposal of the excavated spoil.

Even if a tunnel was started it would have to be completed by later occupants as it was obvious we would not be in residence long enough to see it completed.

It was said that the Kommandant was so convinced that Dulag Luft was escape proof that if a PoW did succeed in breaking out and was subsequently caught and returned to Dulag Luft he would be sentenced to twenty eight days solitary confinement and, on his release, awarded a bottle of champagne. True or false I know not as I did not hear of anyone lucky enough to escape. But it is just the kind of story that could be true.

One afternoon, the tedium was eased by being allowed to play a game of football although with still suffering from the after effects of the sprained ankle, my contribution was limited to hobbling around the pitch and generally getting in the way of the opposing players. Needless to say there were no orange segments at either half time or full time.

On the tenth day we were ordered on parade and issued with a Red Cross food parcel and informed that we were to be transferred to a permanent Camp.

Having been counted and the tally being verified as being correct we were lectured by a German officer to the effect that although it was our duty to escape should any one be caught in the act then the escapee would be shot.

After that it was 'Good luck, attention, right turn, quick march' and out through the gates on our way to the railway station. We did have the courtesy to give an 'Eyes right' as we marched past the officer and he, in return, saluted.

As we marched to the station thoughts centred on the possible destination and the consensus of opinion was that it would be Stalag Luft 6 which was at Memel, on the German/ Lithuanian border and also on the Baltic Coast.

Chapter 12

Destination Unknown

Arriving at the station, to our horror we were confronted with two box cars on the side of which was stenciled '*40 hommes ou 8 chevaux*' which translated as '40 men or 8 horses'.

So that was to be our transport, to be herded together like cattle, thirty-nine prisoners plus two guards per cattle wagon. As we clambered into the box cars our boots were confiscated, no doubt to deter any would be escapees, and the doors were locked. Fortunately, the locking bar allowed the doors to open a couple of inches so that, at least, we were assured of ventilation and also a vestige of light.

As the guards carried machine pistols, any thoughts of overpowering them were completely out of the question. If an attempt to escape was to be made it would have entailed removing floor hoards, basically with bare hands, and it is doubtful whether the noise would have gone un-noticed by the guards.

I was in a more fortunate position that the others in as much that when kitted out, at Dulag Luft, my flying boots were not confiscated so the RAF issue boots were in my kit bag.

We settled down as best we could on the floor which, fortunately, was covered with straw. The guards fared better than us as they each had a stool, but on the other hand we could sleep whereas they had to stay awake.

Late in the day, after much shunting and banging about, to the accompaniment of wheels slipping and the belching of smoke we pulled out of the Yard and steamed into the night.

Sometime during the night we stopped alongside what appeared to be engine sheds but there nothing to indicate our whereabouts. A slave worker brought buckets of hot water so we were able to make a brew of coffee – the American Red Cross parcels included jars of Nescafe and tins of powdered milk with the rather apt name of 'Klim'.

Not having mugs we had to make do with empty food cans. Tin bashing, as it was affectionately known, was to become a way of life as handles for mugs, plates and cooking trays were all fashioned out of empty cans.

Up to now there had not been any question of being let off the train in order to use the toilet, and if taken short it was a case of down wind through the open doorway.

The stop was relatively short and once again we steamed into the night. Daybreak saw us passing through countryside and we made our second stop. Surprise, surprise, we were allowed off the train and seventy-eight men stood alongside the track with our backs to the train and proceeded to urinate. Whilst so engaged, the fact that a passenger train steamed by, going in the opposite direction and with us in full view, did not detract from our relief.

Also it was a welcome relief to stretch one's legs even if it was limited to walking a few yards either way. But the break was short lived, and we were back inside the box cars.

As it was daylight and with my being fortunate to be positioned by the door, at least it was possible to take in the German countryside.

Passing through Eisenach, Erfurt and Weimar it was possible to determine that we had travelled north, from Oberusel, and had then swung eastwards. Obviously we were travelling deeper into the heart of Germany.

In our box car was a member of the Airborne forces who had been captured in Italy and was suffering from acute dysentery. This was not hygienic for the remainder of us as, in addition to excreta, he was passing blood. All he could do was to stuff straw down into the seat of his trousers. In point of fact he should have been in hospital and not on the train. I will add that once we arrived at the Camp he was transferred to hospital and later repatriated.

During the day I offered one of the guards a cigarette which he accepted gratefully. We conversed as best we could, mainly I think due to the similarity of many English and German words. Asking about the machine pistol, he said that it as a Schmeiser and had no hesitation in showing me how it worked. He even allowed me to examine in but, needless to say, under the watchful eye of his counterpart.

After Weimer, during the second night we must have swung north-east as during the following morning we passed through Riesa, which is east of Leipzig, and finally stopped at Mühlbergon-Eloe.

We were ordered out complete with belongings and were given back our boots. After being formed up and counted we were marched away. Those unable to walk were put into a farm wagon which we pulled or pushed.

Soon we were to see our destination, a prison camp in the middle of nowhere and completely devoid of any trees or bushes. The camp was about one mile from Mühlberg village.

The camp turned out to be Stalag IVB, run by the Wehrmacht and with a particularly obnoxious Feldwebel.

The Luftwaffe guards were summarily dismissed and despite protestations that we were RAF personnel and so such should not be imprisoned in an Army Camp, it was of no avail. However, we were informed that we were being held in transit which eased the situation. It was later that we were to discover that 'transit' meant 'permanent'.

Chapter 13

Stalag IVB

After yet another count we were marched to the De-lousing Compound which housed the showers and a gas chamber for clothing.

Later it became apparent that anyone arriving at, or departing from, a Camp, or for that matter admitted to Sick Quarters, was deloused. The fact that you might catch bugs, or lice, within the confines of the Camp was purely incidental; the all important rule was that you were not allowed either to bring them in or take them out.

After two days train journey, the hot showers were like Manna from Heaven but what followed was not. Heads were shaved and armpits and genitals were daubed with a disinfectant which burned like the devil. Looking back, the sight of seventy-eight men clutching themselves and hopping from foot to foot in an attempt to alleviate the excruciating pain may have appeared humorous but at the time, it was anything but.

After retrieving our kit, we were marched to a hut where we were searched in a most arrogant manner. To add insult to injury all the tinned food was pierced, presumably to prevent hoarding.

We were each given a number, mine being 222419, handed a double metallic tag, fingerprinted and photographed. Also, on the back of greatcoats, tunic jackets or battledress blouses a red triangle was stenciled. We were disgusted by this and even more so when we discovered that it was not possible to erase the stencil.

The riot act was read out and after being forced to sign acquiescence we were marched away to a small Compound which contained a single hut and a sack-cloth-screened latrine.

The hut was furnished with three-tier bunks, in rows of two, side by side, and three, front to back, so that eighteen bunks occupied no more than 20 x 6 feet of floor space. The gangway between each double row was restricted to 30 inches.

The bunks occupied half the total floor space and in the other half was a row of tables and benches. To our horror we quickly discovered that the hut was devoid of a washroom and, even worse, a single tap for water.

Having sorted ourselves out and claimed our bunks it was a case of deciding how to occupy the time as we had the remainder of the day before us with nothing to do and nowhere to go.

Fortunately, the decision was delayed by the arrival of lunch which amounted to a bucket of cabbage soup and a bucket of potatoes. All very unappetizing, especially after the way we fared at Dulag Luft.

The soup was virtually hot water with a few bits of white cabbage leaf floating around and the potatoes were boiled in their jackets. The soup rationed out to about one pint and the potatoes to five per person.

Naturally we were feeling somewhat bewildered as we had no idea what next to expect nor how long we would be incarcerated in such conditions.

Automatically we split up into small groups and talked between ourselves. Suddenly I had the bright idea that if there were sufficient empty raisin packets, from the Red Cross parcels, they could be cut down and possibly have sufficient pieces to make a deck of cards. As luck would have it, not only were we able to make a deck of cards, there were sufficient pieces left over to make a set of dominoes.

Within a short space of time we had two foursomes in progress, one playing cards and the other dominoes. With having something with which to occupy the time, the afternoon passed quickly until the next interruption, which became popularly known as 'Bread up'.

Loaves of black bread which rationed out into pieces equivalent to four thin slices, together with a tiny square of what passed as margarine and something round and flat about the size of two ten pence coins which had a light brown exterior, which proved to be rind, and the inside a white mixture containing carraway seeds. We were informed that it was cheese but it was definitely a taste which had to be acquired. Sometime later we discovered it originated from Norway, that the rind was made from raw fish and the white mixture a crumbly cream cheese of somewhat doubtful ingredient. The mint tea did not improve with the addition of sugar and the powdered milk merely went into lumps.

As it was not known when we might receive our next meal, general consensus was to eat only half the bread so that the remainder could be eaten, the following morning, at breakfast. Just as we were finishing eating, some wag called out 'Any one want another slice of this cake before I put it away'.

It was humour such as this that was to maintain our spirits during the privations yet to come and we were to realize that it is the Englishman's sense of humour and ability to laugh at himself that carries him through the adversities of life.

After the meal was finished, the time up to Roll Call was occupied with more cards, dominoes or just plain chin-wagging. At 8 am, to the shout of 'Appel', the unteroffizier entered the hut and after ensuring that none of his charges had gone walkabout, he departed and locked the door behind him.

As dusk approached, we realised we were without another of life's luxuries – artificial lighting – and so once it was too dark to see what we were doing the games were put away and, by degrees, we retired to bed.

The bunks were equipped with a sack-cloth paillasse filled with a mixture of straw and paper shavings and also a couple of thin blankets. It was a case of sleeping in one's under clothes which was not very hygienic as although we did have a change the question of laundering was an unknown quantity as we did not possess any soap.

The following morning we tackled the unteroffizier and it was agreed that we would have the freedom of the compound.

A portrait of Jack Sowter taken early in his RAF career. Jack joined the RAF in October 1941, originally as a trainee wireless operator, but later re-mustered as a navigator and joined the crew of a Handley Page Halifax of 78 Squadron.

Having begun his RAF service at Lord's Cricket Ground, Jack undertook further training at Torquay, Eastbourne, and Dumfries, where he earned his navigator's wings. It was at one of these locations that this group photograph was taken. Jack can be seen in the middle row, second from the right.

Jack Sowter pictured with other crewmembers – he is standing third from the right. He first joined his crew at Lossiemouth and later Marston Moor.

A view of part of Gothenstrasse in Hamburg taken on 1 August 1943, immediately after Operation *Gomorrah*. Note the widespread damage from the recent Allied air raids. (Historic Military Press)

An oblique aerial view of ruined residential and commercial buildings south of the Stadtpark (seen at upper right) in the Eilbek district of Hamburg, Germany. These were among the 16,000 multi-storeyed apartment buildings destroyed by the firestorm which developed during the raid by Bomber Command on the night of 27/28 July 1943. The road running diagonally from upper left to lower right is Eilbeker Weg. (© Crown Copyright/MoD; Courtesy of Air Historical Branch (RAF))

A resident surveys a bomb-damaged street in Hamburg, in the aftermath of Operation *Gomorrah*, on 31 July 1943. (© Crown Copyright/MoD; Courtesy of Air Historical Branch (RAF))

Hamburg under attack during Operation *Gomorrah*. Beginning on 24 July 1943, *Gomorrah* lasted for eight days and seven nights. At the time, it was the heaviest assault in the history of aerial warfare. This photograph was taken during a daylight raid undertaken by the USAAF. (NARA)

A 78 Squadron Halifax II bomber of 78 Squadron pictured at RAF Breighton, Yorkshire, after Operation *Gomorrah*, on 25 September 1943. (© Crown Copyright/MoD; Courtesy of Air Historical Branch (RAF))

An air-to-air shot of another Handley Page Halifax of 78 Squadron that was taken on 25 September 1943. (© Crown Copyright/MoD; Courtesy of Air Historical Branch (RAF))

A view of one part of the Luftwaffe transit camp at Dulag Luft, Oberursel. Like many captured Allied airmen, Jack began his time as a prisoner of war at this camp. It was there that he was reunited with the other three surviving members of his crew. (Historic Military Press)

A view of one of the guard, or watch, towers at Dulag Luft, Oberursel. (Historic Military Press)

Another portrait of Jack, this time taken after his time as a prisoner of war. After he was repatriated to the UK, he served at Church Fenton, Marston Moor, and the Transport Command Development Unit before demobilization in February 1946. Note the Navigator's brevet on his jacket, and the Caterpillar Club pin just below it.

A post-war photograph of Jack dancing with is his wife, Thea.

Dressed up as a Victoria industrialist, Jack, a railway enthusiast, poses for the camera beside his own steam locomotive.

Jack pictured with his first-born great grandson, Dominic, at his home in New Milton, Hampshire, in 2006.

As the days passed so a daily routine evolved. After Roll Call, weather permitting, we would take a turn around the compound which was all of a hundred yards. To relieve the monotony, and change the scenery, we would walk, firstly, in a clockwise direction and then about turn and walk in the anti-clockwise direction. There were no bounds to our ingenuity.

Once back in the hut, between mealtimes, it was the customary cards, dominoes, chin-wagging or sleep. Oh for the luxury of having something to read. It is only when you are without something that you realize how much it can be missed.

The daily soup varied between cabbage, and if you were lucky you might find a minute scrap of meat, possibly horse meat but who cares, swede, turnip, beetroot, pumpkin and sauerkraut. Swede and turnip soup was bad enough and, even now, I avoid both vegetables like the plague but, to me, sauerkraut was the absolute depths. I stomached it because I had to and certainly not from choice.

Cheese was issued one day only each week, as also was an ersatz jam and some kind of liver potted meat but which was quite tasty. Also we received a daily teaspoon of sugar. Ersatz coffee replaced the mint tea each morning, but bread and the small square of margarine was issued only once each day.

Although the Red Cross food parcel was eked out as much as possible, with the meat and fish tins having been punctured there is a limit as to how long they could be kept and soon we were down to the basic rations.

As much as one disliked some of the basic rations, beggars cannot be choosy and especially so as one becomes increasingly more hungry. It was later that we were to learn that the basic ration was exactly the same as for the German guards. One benefit of the Geneva Convention.

Cigarette and tobacco stocks were dwindling and were eked out by taking a few puffs only before extinguishing them. Rolling your own, from the ends, soon became the norm.

One morning, much to our surprise we were ordered outside, complete with kit, and we were convinced the great day had arrived and that we were to be transferred to a Luft Stalag.

Yes, we were being transferred, but not to a Luft Stalag or, for that matter, any other Stalag. Instead of left wheeling and out through the Main Gates it was a case of right wheel and march down the road that ran through the centre of the Camp. We did left wheel but that was halfway down the road and into a large compound, with double gates, containing four large huts and, as we later discovered, the central brick building was a communal latrine. We were allocated the hut at the top of the compound and which bore the number 34B.

Each of the wooden huts was divided into three sections, the two outer sections being living quarters and the centre section a common washroom. At the end of each of the outer sections was an entrance porch complete with door which was locked each night and a single latrine.

The numbering of the Huts did not appear to follow any logical pattern. The top Hut was numbered 34A and 34B, the second 36A and B, the third 43A and B and the fourth 45A and B. The entrance to 'A' was through 'B' and whilst 34, 36 and 43 were equally spaced, the space between 43 and 45 was larger as they were sited either side of the gates.

Each of the living sections contained the usual arrangement of three-tier bunks, tables and benches plus a rectangular shaped brick stove. Each section accommodated 100 men.

The centre section had three rows of sprinklers and two wash basins but, due to lack of pressure, water was only turned on early morning and late evening.

The common latrine was raised several feet above ground level and contained four rows of seats and without any privacy from your neighbour. At the back of the latrine was the collecting pit which was open to the elements and in warm weather attracted an abundance of flies. Periodically one of the Russian prisoners would drive in a tanker pulled by an ox and would hand pump out the pit contents. About half an hour or so later, we would see him spraying the adjoining fields. As you can guess, nothing was wasted.

Roll Call was still twice daily, but with a large compound, weather permitting, it was held outside. Only as the evenings drew in was the second Roll Call held indoors.

Unlike the previous hut we now enjoyed the luxury of electric light although, from time to time, this failed due to someone having attempted to make a small immersion heater and fusing the lights. It did reach the point where the Authorities threatened to cut off the supply completely if the practice did not stop. Needless to say, the practice did not stop, the immersion heaters got better.

One benefit of the larger compound was that walks were less tedious but as further intakes arrived and the other huts became occupied so did the compound become increasingly crowded. Walks tended to last longer and we more than glad of the exercise.

We received another issue of Red Cross food parcels and sufficient to allow one parcel to be shared between two PoWs. As previously all the tinned food was punctured and to which we objected, but to no avail. One could only hope that, at some time in the future, the Germans could be persuaded to change their ways.

As, obviously, there was a stock of Red Cross parcels within the Camp it would appear that British PoWs had been accommodated at Stalag IVB.

It was possible to arrange for the mint tea to be changed to hot water, but even then by the time it was actually issued it was lukewarm so it was not possible to make a decent brew of tea. Also it was pretty hopeless attempting to make porridge.

Another intake arrived, transferred from Stalag VIII-A, and although three, or four, had succeeded in making a dash for freedom, during transit, their freedom was short lived as they were quickly recaptured.

Included in the party were a Canadian Pilot and an Aussie Air Gunner, both of whom had previously been held at Stalag Luft 6. As they had been in captivity longer than we had and, presumably, knew the ropes, it was mutually agreed that they should assume the positions of Leader and Deputy Leader. As such they would become responsible for all negotiations with the Camp Kommandant.

As a protection from the flies, which were a wretched nuisance and particularly to our shaven heads, we were issued with berets. An additional benefit was that we became instantly recognisable to each other. It is surprising how the loss of hair changes one's appearance. Exercise walks gradually formed into groups of two, three or four as friendships developed and resulting, also, in the pooling of resources and when rations were issued, one member collected for his group. The saying that two can eat as cheaply as one could be applied to rations as the food appeared to go further.

This was definitely the case with the Red Cross food parcels. Whilst it was possible, on one's own, to save half a tin of meat it was not possible to do so with a tin of fish. With a groupage, the uneaten meat or fish was always in an un-opened tin.

Thoughts began to turn towards the question of escaping but one of the problems was the lack of tools, i.e. wire cutters. I must admit that I was rather taken aback by the first PoW that I approached on this subject as his reply was that if you think you can make it, good luck to you. Obviously, he was quite prepared to sit it out.

Although we were allowed the freedom of the Compound during daylight, immediately after Evening Roll Call we were locked inside for the night. This was not a problem as the windows opened and it was a simple matter to remove the barbed wire from the outside frame.

The only time a guard was on duty, in the Compound, was during Roll Call, so that in the event of being outside the hut after dark, the only hazard would be the occasional sweep of the searchlight from the elevated Watch Towers.

There was an elevated Watch Tower on each of the four corners of the Camp plus another midway on each side. One of these, unfortunately, was sited on the edge of our Compound. Each Tower, in addition to the searchlight, was equipped with a machine gun and manned by two guards.

During the night, security was increased by guards patrolling outside the perimeter fence but this was on a regular basis and the time interval was quickly determined.

The perimeter fence consisted of two 10-foot-high barbed wire fences and with a single wire, on the ground, running down the centre. Whilst it was the general consensus of opinion that this was an alarm wire it was never put to the test as no one escaped through the double fence. This was due, in part, to the lack of ground cover on the outside of the fence. The only exception was the rifle range which was highly banked but this was only a few yards from the middle Watch Tower on our side of the Camp.

Ten feet inside the perimeter fence was a single strand of barbed wire, some 4 feet above ground, beyond which we were not allowed to stray, the penalty being that we would be shot.

Later when we started ball games this rule was relaxed but theoretically permission was required, from the Watch Tower, before retrieving the ball.

How to get out of the Camp was the problem. Digging a tunnel was discounted due to the distance from the Huts to the perimeter fence, even before considering the overlap required on the outside. Because of the position of the rifle range and the Watch Tower it would not be possible to make a direct line. Bed boards could be used to support a tunnel but getting rid of the spoil would be quite a problem as it could only be disposed of within the Compound.

So it would have to be through the wire and the opportunity would be limited to when the RAF were in the area as then all lights were extinguished. Between our Compound and the next one nearer the Main Gates was a small enclosure which was used as an allotment and tended by French PoWs and as it included a small greenhouse it was thought that it could be used as a staging post.

It would be necessary to cut and re-hook the wire, which was a double lane, between the Compound and allotment, in readiness for an escape bid.

Once outside which direction to take? I decided that unless one headed north to the Baltic ports in the hope of picking up a boat destined for Sweden, it was a long way either west to the Low Countries or south to Yugoslavia. Czechoslovakia and Poland, although much nearer, were treated with suspicion due to the large German population. Also even if one did make contact with the Resistance the possibility of getting back to England appeared somewhat remote.

For better or worse, I decided that in the event of being able to clear the Camp I would head south. My main reasoning was that southwards offered more cover than the flat, open country to the west. I estimated that the journey could be done in about thirty days and that the necessary food supply would be needed as living off the land, especially during the winter months, would be virtually impossible.

Another intake arrived, this time from Dulag Luft, and the resultant increase overflowed into 34A and 36B. Although one looked to see if there was anyone one might know, with shaven heads this was difficult and it was more the reverse as we were wearing berets.

Asking questions as to whether there was anyone from a particular Squadron was treated with suspicion as we had all been informed of the infiltration of stooges. However, if you did find someone from your Squadron suspicion quickly disappeared and also the new intake were soon to realize that they were your only source of news of contemporaries and, possibly more important, keeping up with how the war was progressing.

It was from a member of 78 Squadron that I learned that the Pilot with whom I had done my first Op – Flight Sergeant Jenkinson – had nursed his aircraft home but as the result of crash landing had suffered a broken back. I had flown as his Navigator, due to his own being ill, on the same Operation that our own Skipper did his Second Dickey stint.

I had happened to walk into the Flight Office to be greeted with 'Doing anything tonight?' and having answered in the negative was immediately asked how I felt about doing an 'Op'. Having gulped and asked 'Why me?', the whys and wherefores were explained and with the added rider that you have to start sometime. With what might be called a sickly grin I had no option but to accept. If I had raised any objections no doubt it would have been misconstrued as cold feet and followed with being grounded with the reason being given as suffering from LMF.

Even so when I informed the other crew members I was accused of line shooting and that if I was going anywhere that night it would be to the nearest pub.

I had teamed up with a Welsh Flight Engineer named 'Taffy' Jones but as our cigarettes dwindled so did his apparent enthusiasm in escaping and, hardly surprisingly, it disappeared completely once they dried up completely. When he finally said that he was breaking off the partnership I merely wished him well inwardly thinking that undoubtedly he had found himself a source of cigarettes.

Come what may I decided to continue making plans on my own but fairly quickly found three other similarly minded individuals, by sheer co-incidence from 78 Squadron, with whom to make up a foursome.

Food was now down to the basic German rations and it became noticeable that anyone on their own had difficulty in imposing the necessary self discipline to put aside part of their bread ration for the following day, let alone build up a stock.

However, with being a foursome, each day we were able to set aside a small amount of food and gradually our grub stake was being built. It was a slow process and needed a boost but we could see little likelihood of Red Cross food parcels.

With the shortage of food and the hunger so caused it was small wonder that thoughts turned increasingly towards food and, in particular, to what might have been.

We had a Flight Engineer, an ex-school teacher, from Wolverhampton who had an obsession for steamed jam roly-poly pudding and custard.

After a meal he would take great delight in describing, in great detail, his imaginary pudding which at the onset was the normal pudding-cloth size. But as the days passed so his pudding grew until it was as long as the table and would have needed a sheet in which to be wrapped.

The question of where he would find the vessel in which it could have been cooked just did not enter into the equation.

Adrian Thorne was a Navigator, on Lancasters, and very lucky to be alive. His aircraft had been seriously damaged and was in such a steep dive that, due to the effect of 'g', it was impossible to bail out and Adrian was lying on the floor waiting for the final crash. Suddenly he found himself falling from the sky, pulled his rip-cord and parachuted safely to the ground. He said that he had no recollection of the aircraft disintegrating in mid-air and he was the sole survivor.

Adrian had a theory that if during the drowsy period before finally going to sleep he concentrated on roast chicken, bacon rolls, stuffing, bread sauce, roast potatoes, garden peas and gravy then, providing the concentration was sufficiently intense, he would dream of such a repast. Because the dream would be so realistic, when he awakened he would be convinced that he had partaken of such a meal and all feelings of hunger would disappear.

Whilst being skeptical, no-one could disprove his theory because when all said and done it was all in the mind.

Others talked of steaks, as large as dinner plates, piled high with onions, mushrooms and chips, or plates of bacon and eggs. For myself, thoughts of a meal reflected on what we had at home – the traditional Sunday lunch of roast beef and Yorkshire pudding, or roast pork and apple sauce or roast lamb and mint sauce, to be followed by a fruit pie or pudding. As the pangs of hunger increased, so did the richness of the imaginary meals.

Chapter 14

Autumn

August quietly slipped away into September but although the days were not so hot the sunshine continued.

One morning we were ordered out on parade complete with all our kit. Once again we had high hopes of being moved to a Luft Camp, but again we were disappointed.

The adjoining compound, which previously had been occupied by Russian PoWs, had been evacuated, the inter-communicating gates were opened and we were marched through completely at a loss as to the reason why.

Later in the day the reason became obvious. As the result of the Italian capitulation, the Germans had taken the Italian Armed Forces as prisoners and IV-B was one of the designated reception Camps.

It could be only German logic that could have decided on musical chairs when the obvious solution would have been to have put the Italians in the Russian compound and left us where we were.

The four double huts were totally inadequate for the number of Italians and the excess were housed in hastily erected bivouacs which completely filled the Compound.

To add insult to injury, we were locked in the huts day and night, being allowed out only for Roll Call.

It did not take long to realize that we were not the sole occupants of the huts, as that night bugs bloated with blood came out of the woodwork. Sleep was an impossibility as we were continually waging war on them. We were convinced that if they could have been harnessed, the numbers were such that it would not have presented a problem for them to pull the huts, and occupants, back to England.

The following morning, at Roll Call, vigorous complaints were made but it was two days before the German Authorities reacted.

We were moved into the Compound, being allowed only to take food with us. The huts were then sealed and fumigated. Fortunately, the weather was still fine and sunny so being outside until dusk was not a problem.

That night, as a precaution in case anyone was affected by any lingering traces of gas in the bedding, a night watch was instituted but fortunately, the night passed without incident. That, thankfully, was the last we saw of the bugs.

As my hair was beginning to grow, the beret was becoming less of a necessity and when one of the new intake offered ten cigarettes as payment I had no hesitation in accepting. This was my introduction into the barter system, which was to become very much part of our life style.

After being on the basic ration for a month, Red Cross food parcels began to arrive. Initially the delivery was sufficient only for an issue of one parcel between two PoWs but quite soon we were each receiving a parcel each week.

The parcels originated from Britain, either from the English or Scottish Red Cross, Canada, New Zealand and America. From time to time instead of an individual parcel we had an issue from the bulk supplies received from the Argentine.

Each parcel weighed 10lbs and contained tinned meat, either Corned Beef or Spam, salmon, sardines, tea and cocoa or coffee, powdered or condensed milk, butter or margarine, raisins, porridge oats, jam, sugar and chocolate. Separately there was an issue of cigarettes or pipe tobacco.

No doubt due to the frequency that parcels were now issued, coupled to the ever increasing number of British PoWs, the practice of puncturing tins was discontinued and this allowed the possibility of stock-piling food.

Shortly after the arrival of the Italians, intakes of British and South African Army personnel began to arrive. These were prisoners captured in the North African campaigns and previously imprisoned in Italy. Undoubtedly after the capitulation of Italy they expected to be back home within a relatively short space of time and it must have been very galling to find the Italian guards replaced by the Wehrmacht and then transported to Germany.

Most of the early arrivals were Privates, Lance Corporals or Corporals and were in the Camp only as long as it took the German Authorities to arrange Kommandos, or work parties.

Nevertheless, it did give the opportunity to chat to them and I was fortunate in finding several who came from my neighbourhood. With having been PoWs for up to a couple of years some of them were well kitted out and when items of clothing were offered they were gratefully received. One item other than clothing that I received was a pair of pliers, rather well used but hopefully still good enough to cut through the barbed wire.

Although Kommandos were being dispatched quite rapidly, as the numbers of the Army increased accommodation became more and more of a problem. But with typical German efficiency the problem was solved by the mass evacuation of the Italians.

The bivouacs stood empty in a deserted compound and an escape plan was hurriedly put together. The plan was after Evening Roll Call to wait until it was dark and then to leave the hut via the Barrack Chief's window, which was screened from the remainder of the hut interior. Once outside we would then cut through the barbed wire in order to gain access to the Italian Compound and the safety of the bivouacs. By using the bivouacs as a screen against the searchlight sweeps we would be able to reach the perimeter fence at a point roughly mid-way between the two Watch towers. Then once the patrol had passed by we would cut through the inner and outer wires, taking care to avoid the alarm wire.

Once outside it was decided that it would be safer to crawl the first 20 or 30 yards before making a dash for freedom. This was to be done with our boots tied round our necks in order to reduce any possible noise.

Alas, as had been said by Robbie Burns, 'The best laid plans of mice and men oft go agly'. And indeed so did our plans.

During the afternoon, much to our disgust, a squad of Russian PoWs under German supervision removed the bivouacs and we were back to square one.

The only consolation of the departure of the Italians was that we returned to our original compound and I was back in 34B.

However my sojourn was to be interrupted for a couple of weeks as I was taken ill with laryngitis which put me in Sick Quarters. No doubt it was fortunate that the escape plan had failed otherwise if it had occurred whilst on the run, the result might have been disastrous.

By degrees life within the Camp became more organised and included the formation of an official Escape Committee. After discussing our plans with the Leader, our group were included on the list and now it was a case of sitting and waiting for our names to gravitate to the top of the list.

It was during the waiting period that the foursome became a twosome as the other two decided to drop out.

At last towards the end of October our two names gravitated to the head of the queue and we were informed that our attempt was 'on'.

Restrictions had been relaxed, resulting in our being allowed to remain out of doors until ten o'clock in the evening. What was a bonus was that the Evening Roll Call was still held at eight o'clock. Also it meant that as the days shortened we were still in the Compound after dark.

The plan was that after Roll Call we would put on our greatcoats, so enabling the escape packs to be concealed.

Then whilst the Compound guard was distracted we would worm our way through to the grass patch between the side of the hut and the double lane of wire fencing separating the Compound from the adjacent allotment. The garden was to provide a limited amount of cover across to the perimeter fence.

However, Lady Luck was not kind to us as, having cut through the first fence, the pliers were not man enough to cut through the second fence into the allotment. We had no option but to abort but, on the way back, the cut wire was hooked up in readiness for the second attempt.

The following day was spent in feverishly attempting to sharpen the pliers and that night we made a further attempt. But again we were faced with disappointment. We did gain access to the allotment and managed to reach the perimeter fence without being detected, but again the pliers were not up to the job and for the second time we were forced to abort.

After a lengthy discussion with the Leader it was decided that it would be too risky to attempt the perimeter fence in two halves which, in effect, is what it would entail with the pliers being so ineffective,

Attempting to climb the fence was completely out of the question but as a possible alternative we did discuss the pros and cons of a shallow trench beneath each of the two lanes. This would mean scooping to a depth of 2 feet as we moved forward and scattering the earth behind us.

Whilst we could not foresee any problem in burrowing under the first fence, we had no idea as to how long it might take. It would be necessary to pull back each time the patrol approached and in attacking the second fence the alarm wire could present quite a hazard. So very reluctantly it was decided to put the attempt into cold storage until either effective wire cutters could be obtained or we could come up with an alternative means of exit.

Kommandos were still leaving the Camp but although we made numerous attempts to exchange identities it was not possible to find someone who was prepared to co-operate.

With the allotment now being accessible I decided that it could be used to advantage and I made several nocturnal excursions in order to obtain some fresh vegetables, varying the patch so that the losses would not be too noticeable.

However one night I was extremely lucky as having entered the middle lane I was caught in the searchlight sweep but by flattening myself as much as possible alongside the fence I managed to escape detection. After what seemed to be an age but in reality was possibly less than a minute, the beam swung away and I was able to re-trace my steps.

What I did not realise until I had reached the safety of the shadow of the hut was that, in addition to the guards in the Watch Tower, there were two guards standing less than 30 yards away by the corner of the nearest hut in the next Compound.

Back in the hut I decided that however nice fresh vegetables may be my nocturnal visits were at an end. Winter was now approaching and with it the weather slowly deteriorated and it was decided, with great reluctance, that sleeping rough was not all that might be desired and so thoughts of escaping would need to be shelved until the spring.

Chapter 15

Winter

For reasons not known there was a general change around of hut occupancy and I was to find myself domiciled in 45B which whilst a resident of Stalag IVB was to be, more or less, my permanent 'home'.

At the same time we were allowed the freedom of the Camp which allowed us to inter-mingle with the other Nationals, although we avoided contact with the Russians. The Russian Government were not signatories to the Geneva Convention, which was made abundantly clear by the treatment they received from the German Authorities.

Although the curfew had been extended to ten o'clock, after Evening Roll Call we were confined to our respective Compounds and the gates locked.

As the result of the inter-mingling, I learned that a new intake of Dutch PoWs included several who had civilian clothes in their possession.

As this appeared to be an opportunity too good to be missed I began making enquiries and eventually found a small number who were my height and build and quite happy to trade.

The net result of my business transactions was that in exchange for my RAF issue battle-dress and greatcoat I received a suit and raincoat. Additionally, with cigarettes as payment, I obtained a shirt and tie.

Surreptitiously my spoils were transferred to 45B and hidden beneath my palliasse. Now if I did succeed in breaking out I would not be in uniform and consequently less conspicuous.

Army personnel were continually arriving from Italy, including several who, after the Italian capitulation, had escaped captivity and had joined up with the Partisans before being subsequently recaptured.

From one of them I was able to obtain a grey, herringbone tweed overcoat in exchange for the raincoat plus a blanket. If my escape was during the winter, or early spring, I would now be better equipped to battle against the elements.

Amongst the newly transferred PoWs I came across 'Ginger' Dixon who, prior to joining the Army, was a policeman from my hometown and who lodged in the house next door but one.

I remembered him not only for the colour of his hair but also for the two occasions when he saw fit to reprimand me for transgressions against the law.

The first occasion was during the blackout when he stopped me for riding my bicycle without a light and for which he gave me a ticking off.

The second occasion was when instead of stopping at a 'Halt' sign I merely slowed down and dragged one-foot along the ground. Of course, he had to be there and I, unfortunately, did not see him. Having been stopped he gave me what I considered to be the worst form of punishment – in broad daylight and in full view of several onlookers I was made to re-approach the 'Halt' sign, stop and dismount before being allowed to proceed. Such was the indignity meted out.

With the ever-increasing number of British prisoners, various Camp activities were organized and which started with talks, in the huts, after Roll Call. One was by Terry Hunt, a film cameraman who was shot down on a daylight, low-level Boston sweep over the French coast.

Terry was not actually in the Forces, being employed by the Ministry of Information, but was given the status of Sergeant to cover any eventualities. The aircraft crash landed and the Luftwaffe retrieved the camera intact and Terry was shown the developed film showing the shooting down and the actual crash landing.

Before the war he was a cameraman with one of the British film studios and he regaled us with an insight into both the serious and humorous side of the industry dressed which included a very descriptive account of how Madeline Carroll, dressed in a crinoline gown, had visited the loo!

A South African formed a 'touring' theatrical company – touring by virtue of presenting the plays in the huts as opposed to a theatre. The plays were presented in 'radio' format, complete with sound effects, with the cast behind a screen and reading direct from the script.

As the performances were presented in the 'B' section of the huts, the audience was augmented by the occupants from 'A' and, dependent on the production, by outsiders as well so that the audience could be upwards of 200.

This particular evening the production was Noel Coward's *Cavalcade* and the 'house' was packed with the audience occupying every single square inch of available floor space.

The lights went out and as the play unfolded you could feel the building up of emotion. Not a sound came from the audience, not even someone lighting a cigarette.

As the play ended, instead of the customary 'You have been listening to …' the leading player immediately continued with John O'Gaunt's immortal speech from Shakespeare's *Richard the Second*, Act 2, Scene 1:

> This royal throne of kings, this scepter'd isle,
> This earth of majesty, this seat of Mars,
> This other Eden, demi-paradise,
> This fortress built by Nature for herself,
> Against infection and the hand of war,
> This happy breed of men, this little world,
> This precious stone set in the silver sea,
> Which serves it in the office of a wall.

The atmosphere was now electric as he continued:

> Or as a moat defensive to a house,
> Against the envy of less happier lands,
> This blessed plot, this earth, this realm, this England.

So the hut erupted with thunderous applause and, as the National Anthem was strictly '*verboten*', the spontaneous and tumultuous singing of *There'll Always be An England*.

Could there ever be any doubt as to the final outcome of this war other than ultimate victory for the Allied Forces?

A number of Army musicians, transferred from the Italian PoW camps, had been allowed to retain their instruments and they formed the first of the IVB bands, giving concerts of popular music, during the evenings, in the huts.

With them was a vocal trio who included *Lily Marlene* in their repertoire and which they always sang in German and as a marching song. It sounded far superior to the versions I heard after the war when it was crooned by the likes of Anne Shelton.

Following protracted negotiations with the German Authorities agreement was reached for the conversion of one of the Army huts to a theatre and which, on Sundays, could be used by all denominations as a Church.

The Authorities co-operated in the conversions and also turned a blind eye to the bartering carried out in order to obtain items not available through the auspices of the Red Cross.

Once the theatre opened it always played to packed houses but, one could say, they were fortunate in having a captive audience. Certainly no one objected to paying the cigarette admission charges.

German officers and senior NCOs were present for most of the productions and in some of the comedy shows had to stand a certain amount of ribbing, but whether they saw through all of the double meanings is another matter.

The first production was staged just before Christmas and in the New Year, in addition to the Theatre company, the theatre was used for the staging of musicals and the Mühlberg Symphony Orchestra, which was formed, and conducted, by Alan Bolt. Their solo pianist was an ex-cinema organist from Newcastle upon Tyne.

One of the stage productions had, as leading 'lady', a Canadian who was ex-78 Squadron and included a strip tease which he enacted slowly and seductively until he stood clad in just a pair of 'long johns' adorned with a green rosette over his crotch. Suddenly a cry from the audience of 'How Green is my Valley' brought down the house and, momentarily, stopped the show. I do believe it was not stage managed as others who had seen the show earlier did not say that it had happened during their performances.

The advent of the theatre and all forms of entertainment had a considerable effect in raising morale.

Because the Germans had started spot checks for contraband I decided that under the palliasse was not the best of places for my civilian clothes and that a new hiding place had to be found. Fortunately the problem was solved quickly and easily following a chat with the Theatre Wardrobe Manager who was more than happy to oblige. In exchange for the use of the clothes he agreed that they would be available as and when my need arose.

One of the biggest boosts to morale was the arrival of the first letters from home, which were read and re-read until they started to disintegrate at the creases.

We were now allowed to write one letter and one postcard each month, which meant that in addition to writing to my mother I could also write to my girlfriend.

One day the *Mühlberg Times* appeared, which was a hand printed single sheet. A copy was produced for each of the British Compounds and was hung in rotation in each of the huts. This was followed later by a second newspaper published by the South Africans. The newspapers were made up of feature articles but also included tit-bits gleaned from letters from home.

As winter progressed so the weather deteriorated and our out of doors activities were severely curtailed and we were reduced to 'in house' occupations.

The song may say 'It's a long, long time from May to December' but in the first year of captivity October to March seemed even longer.

A daily supply of fuel, in the form of coal briquettes, was provided but was sufficient only for cooking. Heating was a different proposition and as the days became colder we looked for additional sources of fuel.

Initially we seized the obvious and proceeded to burn our bed-boards but even that had a limit when the numbers were reduced to the extent that sleeping became more of a balancing act.

Reluctantly the German Authorities delivered loads of coal dust to the Compounds and with the addition of water we were able to make them into balls about the size of a large cricket ball. By allowing them to dry out, and strangely enough they did not disintegrate, they were used to augment the briquettes, crude but effective. This was one fatigue for which there was not a shortage of volunteers.

With each hut having to provide a fatigue party to collect the daily briquette supply, the location of the fuel store was known and it was not long before raiding parties became a nightly occurrence. But these came to an abrupt halt when, one night, a raiding party was caught in the act. Unfortunately, one of them decided to run for it, but was shot and killed.

The PoW was Taffy Jones, with whom I had formed a twosome when we first arrived at IVB.

During December, the Authorities offered to allow a fatigue party, under escort, to take two hand-drawn farm wagons into the neighbouring forest in order to collect fire wood and I volunteered for one of them.

We were formed up at the Main Gate, counted and then escorted a few miles into the forest. On the return journey we came in through the gates at the bottom of the Camp and were not counted. This seemed too good to be true and I decided that if this was common practice then, winter or no, it would provide the way out.

Alas, subsequent parties left and returned through the Main Gates and, additionally, were counted.

The winter months passed with the days occupied with reading, playing Bridge or Chess or chin-wagging. If the weather was kind then I could take a daily walk. A complete circuit inside the perimeter fence was estimated to cover one mile and the norm was six circuits in the morning and six circuits in the afternoon.

The purpose of the walks was two fold, to relieve the boredom but, more importantly, to keep in shape in readiness for an escape. Evenings were covered by the occasional visit to the theatre or with in-house entertainment.

Over Christmas the curfew was lifted, which enabled the Church to celebrate Midnight Communion on Christmas Eve and again on New Year's Eve.

As 1943 slipped away and 1944 dawned we wondered if it would herald the bright New Year for which we hoped, but only time would tell.

Chapter 15

Spring

Winter blossomed into spring and with it improvement in the weather. It is said that in the spring a young man's fancy turns to love, but not when he is in a Prisoner of War Camp.

Following negotiations with the Authorities an additional hut was erected within the RAF Compound which was to be used partly as a library and partly for Educational purposes with ex-school teachers providing tuition covering a wide range of subjects.

Thanks to the Red Cross, textbooks were obtained and it was possible to study up to degree standard but I do not know if anyone sat an external examination or used the knowledge gained to assist in further studies after the war.

The library was stocked with books supplied by the Red Cross, from PoWs who had brought them from the Italian PoW Camps and from recipients of Book Parcels, from home, who passed them on once they had been read.

With the advent of increased numbers of Canadians and Americans a second band was formed who played the music of Glenn Miller, Tommy and Jimmy Dorsey, Duke Ellington, Benny Goodman, etc.

They had a trumpet player by the name of Goodman, no relation to Benny, who could make the trumpet virtually talk and his solos were always greeted with rounds of applause.

A South African wrote the musical *Mühlberg Melodies of 1944* and which included such numbers as *Do you love me or is it just the medals* which was sung by a Guardsman to his girlfriend, *I'm Bedalia for Ismalia the fan dance queen* sung, naturally, by the dancer complete with fans, a ballad called *Darling Patricia you're the one for me* and a cowboy song which started 'I'm a long, long way from the folks at home' and ended with 'and then I get to dreaming'.

It was a huge success and there were many of us that felt that it would not have disgraced the London stage had it been put on at the end of the war.

With the arrival of sports equipment, again through the auspices of the Red Cross, soccer, rugby, basketball, volleyball and softball teams were formed. Pitches were marked out in the Army Compounds and Inter-hut matches were played.

By degrees these extended to International matches with the Home Countries playing soccer and with rugby extending to the Australians, New Zealanders and South Africans. It was not long before the International soccer matches included the Dutch and French teams.

At one game against Holland, before the start of the match the spectators were entertained by the Dutch Army band who, in defiance of a number of Germans present, immediately before the kick-off played the National Anthems of both countries.

During one of the Inter-hut games, one of the goal keepers drop-kicked the ball high and long. The opposing goal keeper was standing arms folded, legs crossed, leaning up against the right hand, facing, goal post. He never moved except to unfold his arms and catch the ball as it dropped into his hands.

A running track was marked out and in addition to my daily walks I started to sprint 200 meters and returned what to me seemed to be a respectable time of 23 seconds.

One day, after completing the usual 200 metres and still feeling comparatively fresh, I decided to double the distance to 400 metres and surprised myself with a time of 59 seconds. From then on the 200 metres was dropped in favour of the longer distance and eventually I reduced the time to 53 seconds.

By now the PoWs had split up into various factions.

There were those who studied and those who tutored. There were those who provided the Camp entertainment, either in the glare of the footlights or back stage. There were those who played sport or took part in athletics. There were those who were prepared to escape and those who helped to make it possible. Sadly, there were also those who were quite content to sit around and wait for the war to end.

In preparation for an escape a food supply was essential and in order to stockpile I decided to forego cigarettes so that they could be exchanged for chocolate. Additionally, if the food parcel included coffee it would be drunk black or, if it contained tea then it was drunk un-sweetened so enabling the milk and sugar to be exchanged for chocolate.

Slowly the stock was amassed and when New Zealand parcels containing Army ration vitamin enriched chocolate were issued, I offered Canadian chocolate in exchange. There was a bit of carrot dangling in the offer as the Canadian chocolate was milk whereas the New Zealand was plain. Although the weight was the same the Canadian bar was larger but, of course, not as thick so psychologically it appeared more.

The only refusal came from a Canadian, with no thoughts of escaping but who thought he would try the New Zealand chocolate for a change.

Cigarette and clothing parcels were starting to arrive. The former contained 200 cigarettes and my first clothing parcel included a blanket and a pair of black leather shoes.

Eventually the stage was reached when I was ready to take the plunge. My stockpile included sufficient chocolate for twenty-eight days, i.e. twenty-eight bars, 200 cigarettes and a German-made wick-type lighter.

The Escape Committee which was now under new leadership was contacted and as the result of the discussions my name was added to the list. Naturally I was not given any indication as to how long the waiting period might be.

Searches became more frequent and as I could not afford for my hoard to be discovered it was spread between several trusted friends. The fact that an individual might have a few bars of chocolate in his possession was generally over-looked but if the particular guard carrying out the search decided otherwise then only a few bars were lost and they were easily replaceable. From time to time the guards were given sweeteners and another ploy was to deliberately leave something lying around for them to pick up.

Some of the would-be escapees changed places with Privates and went out on Kommandos. Having heard that in the IV Area Kommandos were working mainly in salt mines and sugar beet factories I was not enamoured and preferred to wait in the queue. A farm Kommando would have been a different proposition but that appeared to be out of the question.

As more and more cigarette parcels arrived it was inevitable that inflation should creep into the bartering system and, unfortunately, it was the Canadians and Americans who were the main culprits as their parcels contained 1,000 cigarettes as opposed to our 200.

The Black Market was flourishing and providing you had the necessary chocolate, coffee or cigarettes there was virtually nothing you could not buy. At no time was it more evident than when the guards were due to go on leave.

Each evening, after Roll Call, the BBC news was read out in each of the huts. Whether the radio was homemade or from the Black Market is not known. Suffice to say it was continually moved around to avoid discovery.

On the morning of 6 June we heard the news which was long awaited – D-Day. The invasion of France was under way and there was wild speculation as to how long the war would now last. No one imagined that it would be another eleven months before the German Army would finally surrender.

Chapter 17

Summer

As spring gave way to summer so did soccer and Rugby give way to cricket and athletics. Cricket matches started between Hut teams followed by Inter-compound matches and finally Test Matches between England, Australia, New Zealand and South Africa.

The Canadians and Americans continued with softball, volleyball and basketball, and had to put up with quite a lot of ribbing as we referred to softball and basketball as the girls' games of rounders and netball.

At Bridge I was partnered by Warrant Officer Atkinson who was a Glider Pilot captured during the Sicily landings.

We played copious Rubbers against two Army Sergeants, and it was just as well that we were not playing for stakes as, invariably, we were on the losing side.

However, on one occasion I was dealt a hand to remember. The Ace, King, Queen and Jack of Hearts, the Ace, King, Queen and a small Diamond, the Ace, Queen and a small Club and the King and a small Spade.

Without hesitation I opened the bidding with a strong No trump which brought the reply of 'Two Spades' and no intervening bids. Two No-trumps was answered with 'Two Spades'.

Convinced that my partner must have the Ace of Spades and that a Slam was in the offing, I called for Aces and was horrified by the reply of 'Five Clubs' signifying that the Ace of Spades was not there. I was stuck with five of something and somewhat bravely made a final bid of

Five Hearts which was doubled immediately by the player on my left and followed by two 'No bids' and to which I added a third.

The opening lead was the Ace of Spades whereupon my Partner laid down Dummy, rose from the table and disappeared immediately to the loo!

There it was in all its glory, the bare Ten of Hearts supported by seven Spades to the ten, Jack, Queen, small Clubs to the Jack and three small Diamonds. Five Hearts between us and eight against and the distribution just had to be five and three, if not six and two with being doubled.

The first trick was lost but I won the second and then decided that the only sensible thing to do was to draw trumps and then play a No-trump hand. Miraculously the trumps were evenly distributed – four in each hand.

The Jack of Clubs was lost to the King and after that it was plain sailing as I had all the Master cards. Five Hearts made and doubled plus the bonus of 100 Honour points.

At least twice a week I would bundle my blankets and clothing under my arm and take myself up to the De-lousing Compound. Not because of livestock but simply to get a hot shower and it was quite sometime before I was rumbled and refused entry.

The alternative to a hot shower was, each evening, to stand naked in the Washroom, sluice down with a bucket of cold water, soap all over and then rinse off with a second bucket.

One day I was informed by the Escape Committee Leader that with the co-operation of the French they had been able to establish an escape route and outside assistance. It was made quite clear that it was an expensive operation due to the sweeteners demanded by the French and any help would be appreciated. As I was receiving cigarette parcels fairly regularly I poured some 1,200 cigarettes into the organisation.

The route started with a 'hide' near the Camp followed by a Contact some 20 kms distant who would guide you to the Marshalling Yard and help you into a 'sealed' box-car which he would then re-seal.

Because of the changed route, I decided to exchange my civilian clothing for Army trousers and shirt, a French Army tunic and a pair of blue overalls.

A rival Committee had been formed whose plan was to dig a tunnel starting from beneath the Educational Hut. If successful it was their intention to take advantage of our route thereon and which would have completely blocked both the 'hide' and the contact's facilities.

Quite frankly I could not see their Leader getting very far as he was well over six feet tall and, consequently, stuck out like the proverbial sore thumb.

I was playing Chess, on a regular basis, with a London Schoolboys ex-champion and quite naturally being beaten on a regular basis but, at least, I was learning all the time.

On one of the few occasions that I did succeed in scoring a win he must have had his thoughts anywhere but on the game as to my sheer astonishment he fell for 'Fool's Mate'.

With the French now being actively involved in the escape plans, I was introduced to Henri – their Liaison Officer – and, through him, to several of the French PoWs. This resulted in spending quite some time in their company and as they insisted that only French should be spoken, my limited schoolboy French broadened to the point that I was thinking in French and not having to continually resort to mental double translations. My grammar left much to be desired but, that apart, I became quite fluent. The high spot was, one evening, being taken to their own theatre and having no difficulty in following the dialogue.

Each morning small groups of French PoWs left the Camp, on parole, to work in and around Mühlberg village with one group working in the Cemetery.

Additionally, each afternoon a party of eight French PoWs, including Henri, accompanied by a guard went down to the Cemetery. On several occasions I was given the opportunity to be included. Fortunately my being included was not detected mainly, I believe, because the guards were concerned with numbers and not faces and coupled with the fact that it was not always the same guard and the French, also, changed the bodies in the party.

The highlight of these afternoons out was on the return journey as, quite often, a stop would be made in the village for a beer.

On several occasions we were heartened by the sight of vapour trails from hundreds of American B17, B29 and B24 bombers on their way to Berlin. At the onset, we were herded indoors but once it was realised that we could still watch from the windows we were allowed to remain outside.

One Monday morning one of the bombers was hit and we watched a crew member descending by parachute and landing within 200 metres of the Camp.

He may have had an early breakfast at an airfield in East Anglia, but he had lunch in the Camp hospital and had received his first Red Cross food parcel. Unfortunately, he had suffered a broken leg, on landing, but within a couple of weeks he was out of Hospital and hobbling around on crutches.

One evening, at Roll Call, we were treated to a humorous diversion due entirely to someone attempting an escape earlier in the day and it being necessary to cover for him. The usual arrangement was for a small person to position himself, at Roll Call, in the rear rank towards the end from which the count was started. Then after being counted to crouch down and dodge to the opposite end. As the Roll Call was in the hut it made the switch a lot easier.

The count was made and the number was correct, but the German unteroffizier was not satisfied and had a recount. The procedure was repeated, the number again was correct but the unteroffizier was still not satisfied. So we had a second recount followed by a fourth and each time the number was correct. Undaunted, the unteroffizier decided to call the 'register' and quite naturally he had a 100 per cent reply.

The unteroffizier then smiled and calmly thanked us for our co-operation but unfortunately our efforts had been wasted as Sergeant … had been caught trying to tag on to the end of a fatigue party as it was going through the Main Gate and with that we were dismissed and bidding us 'Goodnight', he departed.

It would appear that there was a Luftwaffe airfield somewhere in the vicinity as we had several low-level sweeps, by a Ju88, over the Camp and mainly on a Sunday evening.

One particular Sunday, he made an even lower pass, too low in fact, as when he pulled out and started his climb the tail dropped resulting in the tail wheel hooking on to the barbed wire fence. Fortunately, he gave the motors full boost and he got away with it but not before uprooting a couple of stakes supporting the barbed wire. The tail wheel broke free and to loud cheers he disappeared into the blue.

Needless to say that was the last we saw of him but a rumour did circulate that he was an oberstleutnant and that he had been grounded for his misdeeds.

It was during my waiting period that what could be called The German Baiting Season evolved as it was something that was most definitely not pre-planned.

Morning Roll Call was held at eight o'clock and at five minutes to eight the Army, in the adjoining Compound, would be on parade and fully dressed.

We would endeavour to be outside by eight o'clock even if still in pyjamas with either a greatcoat or battle dress blouse on top. Inevitably some would still be inside and would be rousted out by the guards, sometimes with help of a rifle butt.

We were not deterred by this and if anything, it made some of us more determined to peacefully resist by even being in bed when the guards entered the hut. Also, the numbers of protesters gradually increased.

The German answer to this was that having held Roll Call we would be kept on parade for an extra half an hour. But we were not deterred.

Each morning was the same and the thirty minutes stretched to forty-five minutes and then to sixty minutes.

As the punishment had failed to have any effect, the tactics were changed. Instead of total dismissal they introduced what to us was a childish practice of dismissing in dribs and drabs with the unteroffizier deciding who should go and who should stay.

This ploy failed miserably due to those of us not having been dismissed taking things into our own hands and when the opportunity could be seized of dashing, zig-zag fashion, the 50 yards, or so, to the safety of the huts.

It did not take the Authorities too long to realise they were on a losing wicket and the extended Roll Calls were discontinued. We in turn, honour satisfied, condescended to be on parade at the appointed time.

The other fact which helped with our peaceful protest was that we were not going anywhere and as long as we were kept on parade so, also, had the guards to be present.

It was common practice that on dismissal there would be a mad dash for the huts in order to be first in the queue for the breakfast brew.

One morning, having been dismissed, and for once ahead of the Army, I decided to take a walk before having breakfast. Having crossed into the Army Compound I was just about level with the first hut when the 'Dismiss' whistle blew. A rugby scrum was nothing to the surge that hit me with such force that I was lifted bodily and my feet did not touch the ground before being deposited in the hut.

At last my name reached the head of the queue and I was informed that, weather permitting, I was earmarked for the following morning.

Chapter 18

A Taste of Freedom

The great day had dawned with a cloudless sky and promised to be another hot day so there was no possibility of the projected escape bid being cancelled.

On two days each week a fatigue party of some fifty British PoWs, escorted by several guards, were allowed to take two farm wagons into the neighbouring woods in order to gather fire wood. It was from one of these excursions that myself and two other PoWs were scheduled to escape.

We were issued with spare identity discs and as the fatigue party would be searched before leaving the Camp it was arranged that our escape packs would be carried out by one of the French fatigue parties who, presumably because they were on parole, enjoyed the luxury of not being searched.

Knowing that I was destined to escape I had left my pack, containing food and cigarettes together with the French Army tunic and the overalls, with Joe – the Escape Committee Leader.

We were briefed that the escape attempt was to be made on the return journey as the fatigue party would be re-counted after the wood had been collected and immediately before starting back.

In order to make up the discrepancy in numbers when the fatigue party arrived back at the Camp it was arranged that spare bodies would be waiting in the '*vorlage*'. This was permissible as, fortunately, the Camp Post Office was opposite to the Guard Room. On being given the necessary signal the applicable number of bodies would infiltrate into the fatigue party before the final count was made.

The fatigue party, after being counted, split into two sections, each section further splitting up so that some pulled from the front whilst the remainder pushed from the sides and rear of the wagons.

The wagons were trundled some 4 miles from the Camp, including crossing the railway line, before being halted and given the order to collect brushwood. Once the wagons were filled we were allowed time for a breather and a smoke and, naturally, the guards were not slow in accepting cigarettes that were offered. At no time did I find a German who refused any tidbit that was offered.

It was during the rest period that we were given our final briefing. It was explained that after crossing the railway line the track narrowed and that there were bushes either side that provided excellent ground cover. This would be the spot where we would make our break and the remainder of the fatigue party would provide the necessary screening and, if required, a minor diversion.

Cigarettes finished, we were counted and with the guards satisfied that they had not lost any of their charges we started the return journey and with the wagons being loaded the pace was slower than when empty.

After crossing the railway line we took up our positions on the left side of the wagons and as we approached the narrow point the PoWs to the front and rear edged outwards in order to obscure the guards' vision. Immediately we were given the signal we dived into the undergrowth, watching the column pass by and the PoWs resuming their original positions.

As a passenger train steamed over the level crossing we took advantage of the cover provided and dashed smartly to the other side of the track, but a quick glance showed that the fatigue party had been halted some 200 to 300 yards further along the track.

We thought that our absence had been noticed and we flattened ourselves amongst the tree and bushes. However they must have stopped for a breather because after a short break the fatigue party resumed its journey back to Camp.

After waiting a further ten minutes we raced across the railway line and buried ourselves in a reasonably dense wood with plenty of ground cover.

It was now a case of waiting until dusk before setting off to Mühlberg village and, in particular, the Cemetery. Whilst we were waiting the only sign of movement was a solitary deer which we were quite content to watch until it finally moved away. If we had moved it could have been disturbed and in dashing away it might have drawn attention to our presence should there have been any one in the wood.

With the arrival of dusk we stretched our limbs, dusted ourselves down and set off towards Mühlberg, reaching our objective without incident and settling down for the night.

It was my first experience of being in a Cemetery after dark and for quite some time it seemed somewhat eerie but eventually I dozed off into a fitful sleep. With not posing the question to my two companions I have no idea as to whether they had any misgivings.

The following morning, around eight o'clock, the French parole fatigue party arrived and handed my companions their escape packs. I explained that mine would be brought to the Cemetery, that afternoon, by Henri and his party.

Without any further delay we were taken to Point 'A', which entailed hopping over the wall, running in a crouched position to the far end of the wall and then across the field to the wood on the far side. Point 'A' turned out to be a dugout with the entrance covered with brushwood.

As soon as it was dark my companions left the dugout, replaced the brushwood cover and set off for Point 'B', leaving me the sole occupant.

The next day was Saturday and just after eight o'clock I was collected and taken back to the Cemetery where I was given the task of peeling potatoes in readiness for the mid-day meal.

It was just as well that I was so occupied as, during the morning, there was a Military funeral after which one of the firing party came into the hut. He spoke to me in French and my reply apparently satisfied his curiosity as he rejoined the others and marched back to the Camp.

Henri and his party arrived as usual and I was handed my food and clothing but I was disappointed to learn that Point 'B' was full and that it would be necessary to spend a further night at Point 'A'.

However, after Henri's party had returned to Camp I was taken to the farm, adjacent to the Cemetery, and hidden in the hay loft. After the floor in the hut and, also the dugout, sinking into the hay was sheer bliss.

Sunday was spent at the Cemetery and in the evening, after having been given a loaf of bread and a map, I was escorted back to the hay loft. The Frenchman explained that after memorizing the route to Point 'B' it was essential that the map was destroyed and also that I was not to move out until Monday evening. I was informed that rendezvous time was eight o'clock in the evening, and as the Contact would be there each evening the problem of a missed meeting was completely out of the question.

Monday was spent in memorising the route until I knew it backwards. Point 'B' was at Elsterwerda, to the east of Mühlberg, and the rendezvous was at a garage on the right hand side of the road leading northwards from the town.

As soon as it was dusk I vacated the hay loft and, after making sure that it was safe, crept to the edge of a wood which was separated, by a small track, from a potato field. After taking the opportunity to scrape up a few potatoes I destroyed the map and buried the remains in the hole before replacing the earth and potato top.

In order to distance myself from the farm I walked across the field and found a track on the far side. Seeing the silhouette of a cyclist I dived under cover and waited for him to pass by.

Fortunately, it was a starlight night so, on regaining the track, with the aid of friendly Polaris, it was possible to head due east. In order not to deviate from my direction, I fixed on a point ahead and on reaching that position, rechecked my bearings, fixed a further point and continued on my way. Too many stories had been heard of people walking around in circles and fixing a point ahead was a tip that I had been given.

The journey across country was uneventful until I came to a small river, or possibly a canal, but too wide to jump and possibly, too deep to consider wading across. On a 'Heads you win, Tails you lose' basis, for better or worse, I decided to turn to the right. My Good Fairy was watching over me as, within some hundred yards, I came to a bridge. 'Bridge' was most definitely an overstatement as it was no more than 12 inches wide, made of iron which appeared to be well and truly rusty, and some 3 to 4 feet above the water. As soon as I put my foot on the bridge it started to sway and I was convinced that either I would over balance or it would collapse. Either way there appeared to be the distinct possibility of being dumped, unceremoniously, into the water below. Plucking up courage and with bated breath I went down on my hands and knees and, holding on for dear life, slowly inched across to the opposite bank. Dry land has never been reached so thankfully and I lay on the ground for several minutes before resuming my journey.

After taking a further bearing I carried on and hit the first village 'spot on'. As I approached a farm house a dog began to bark and, in the interests of safety, I did a short detour and regained the road a couple of hundred yards beyond the farmhouse.

Passing through the second village I heard the sound of approaching footsteps but could not see anyone. As there was a low wall between a house and the pavement, I took cover behind it and lay in the shadows. The footsteps gradually came closer, passed by and disappeared into the distance.

Beyond the village, the road came to a 'T' junction where I turned left and crossed the bridge over the river, afterwards taking the opportunity to quench my thirst.

Having skirted a third village, dawn was breaking and, in the distance, it was possible to discern the outskirts of Elstawerda. The immediate problem was to find somewhere to lie up until the evening.

Walking along, I spotted what appeared to be some tall weeds between a small-holding and a ditch and, as there did not appear to be any other cover in sight, I decided that it would have to suffice. Once in the middle I settled down and went to sleep. I had covered some 18 kilometres.

I was awakened by the sound of voices and, by slightly raising my head, it was possible to observe two German civilians talking to each other and, to my consternation, appearing to be looking in my direction. I flattened myself as much as possible and it would appear that the fact they were looking in my direction was purely coincidental as when they had finished their conversation, they both departed.

It was only 9 am and it was going to be a long wait until evening and, judging by the cloudless sky, with the morning sun already raising the temperature, it was going to be another hot day.

Sitting up, my head was below the top of the weeds, although having taken stock of my position the small-holding was more akin to a market garden and the patch of weeds was, in fact, six rows of sweetcorn with me positioned between rows four and five. At least the leaves would afford a certain amount of shelter from the sun. The ditch, which I had seen earlier, separated row six from the next field and a pathway ran alongside row one.

During the morning, I noticed a French PoW ploughing the field and, checking that no one else was around, when he reached the ditch I stood up and succeeded in attracting his attention. He confirmed that it was a market garden and also said the Master was a bit of a so and so and that I would be in for a hard time should he see me.

During the afternoon the Frenchman gave me a call and threw over a bottle of cold coffee which was gratefully received. He explained that the Master usually departed at 6 pm and that it should be safe to move out by 6.30 pm.

As I had not had a drink for sixteen hours, cold coffee tasted delicious and it was drunk very sparingly. Lying there waiting, all one can do is to think and wish that there was something with which to occupy the time.

At about 5.30 pm I could hear the Master screaming at one of his workers and asked myself the question: Why is it that Germans always appear to scream when either angry or over-excited?

By 6 pm all was quiet and peaceful and the Master should have departed. It was just as well that I did not stand up as at a quarter past six the Master walked up between rows five and six, stooping, here and there, to pull out some weeds. How he failed to see me, face down, in the next row will remain one of life's mysteries. But see me he did not and having reached the end of the row, apparently decided to go home.

At 7 pm, somewhat anxiously, I peered all around and, seeing that the coast appeared to be clear, stood up, dusted myself down and after stretching my aching limbs, left my hiding place.

Quickly regaining the road I walked into the town, passing a Russian Lager and the railway station. Not being too sure of my bearings and with not a garage in sight, I stopped a French PoW and entered into a conversation. After explaining who I was he gave me the necessary directions. Thanking him, I retraced my steps, crossed the railway line, carried on up the hill and found the garage at the top.

Although two men could be seen within the grounds, I was not sure of their identity and so held back. After a few minutes a French PoW appeared from across the road and it was he who was the Contact. He said that it would be necessary to hide in the woods and to return at midnight. Also, that he would take care of my haversack.

Although explaining that it was understood that he would provide the necessary cover and that I had paid handsomely into the organization, he was adamant that providing cover was not part of his agreement.

Although there was a track alongside the garage leading towards the wood there were people walking towards the garage and so I decided to continue up the hill and turn into the woods as and when the opportunity arose. Having passed a tall man, with a haversack on his back, walking in the opposite direction I veered off towards the undergrowth. But a voice called after me. It was the tall man and, obviously, something had made him suspicious. Was there a curfew of which I was unaware? I could not think of any other possible reason but, surely, if that was so I would have been informed.

He asked for my pass and, in my best German, I replied that I did not have it with me as I had lost my jacket and my pass was in one of the pockets. He rattled away, in German, much too fast for my limited knowledge and all I could say in reply was that I did not understand.

However, when he said 'Come with me' that I did understand and it was a case of silently admitting defeat and realizing that my taste of freedom was at an end.

Chapter 19

Return to Stalag IVB

Feeling rather disgruntled and disconsolate I was escorted back down the hill and as we passed the garage there was no sign of the Contact. If, as I had been led to believe, the Contact had provided a 'hide' I would not have been in this situation. Most certainly, had I had the benefit of hindsight the number of cigarettes poured into the organisation would have been considerably less.

Just before we reached the railway line we turned left off the main road and, after a few hundred yards, arrived at a small Kommando. After much Heil Hitler-ing and saluting I was handed over to the Wehrmacht guard and the civilian continued on his way. As he was a Party member, judging by the small Swastika in his lapel, no doubt he would be suitably rewarded.

As the guards did not speak English an interpreter was summoned who, when he appeared, was wearing British Army trousers and shirt. Although speaking English, it was with an accent I was unable to place but, in conversation, he said that the members of the Kommando were our Allies. Much to my amazement he added that they were South Africans. To me, South Africans together with Australians, Canadians, New Zealanders, Indians etc. were part of the British Empire and, therefore, were one of us. It was the French, Dutch, Americans etc. that were Allies.

Whist talking to the South African, my eyes wandered round the room and although the window was barred, the spacing was such that it appeared possible to squeeze through and as there was only the one German, if the remainder of the rooms were similar then it should be possible to take my leave in time for the midnight rendezvous.

Unfortunately, after only a short period a second guard appeared with his rifle slung over his shoulder and could only have been in his teens. He was to be my escort.

We ambled back to the main road and then turned left so that we were going further away from the garage and arrived at the Russian Lager that I had passed earlier in the evening.

The guard stopped to speak to another German soldier, who was with his girlfriend, and eventually I was led inside. The guard handed me over to a Feldwebel who was dressed in a 'T' shirt and shorts and I noticed how carefully manicured his hands were with the nails shaped to points. One had heard of homosexuality amongst the German males and the thought passed through my mind that, possibly, he could be that way orientated and that a member of the Hitler Youth could be tucked away somewhere in the background. On the other hand, I could have been doing him an injustice.

Although I was questioned in German it was possible to understand and I handed over my PoW identity disc and disclosed that my name was John Richmond. With a false identity disc, John Richmond seemed as good a name as any, providing, of course, that I did not forget. I added that I was a Sergeant in the RAF and had escaped from Stalag IVB. It was later that I realized that 'in the RAF' should have been omitted.

The Feldwebel then used the telephone, no doubt to inform his superiors that he had an escaped prisoner, from Stalag IVB, in his custody and requesting instructions. No doubt IVB would be informed and they would have great difficulty in reconciling the name John Richmond with the identity disc number. But as far as I was concerned that was their problem.

The Felbwebel asked how the overalls had been obtained and I had no hesitation, untruthfully, in informing him that they had been obtained from one of the camp guards.

A look of sheer incredulity spread over his face. Obviously he was very naive or had been shielded from the facts of life because it was plain to see that, in his eyes, it was incomprehensible that a guard could commit such a crime. He questioned 'A guard, a German guard?'

I assured him that they had, indeed, been obtained from a German guard in return, adding insult to injury, for a payment of forty English cigarettes.

His first turned red and then to purple. The shock had been more than his system could contain and I thought he would collapse with apoplexy. He stood there absolutely speechless and then as what had been said sank in he ranted and raved and it was all I could do not to smile. Although extremely difficult I did manage to maintain a straight face even though it did entail biting my bottom lip.

After he had quietened down and regained his composure I asked if I might have some water. The request was refused but I did not feel that the accompanying tirade was justified. Turning to the guard, the Feldwebel gave instructions as to my immediate destination and we departed.

As we walked, as opposed to marching, through the town twilight was giving way to darkness and when we reached the far side and came to an intersection I suggested, with my tongue firmly in the side of my cheek, that we part company and he could say, when questioned, that I had escaped under cover of darkness before he could unsling and raise his rifle. Needless to say the request fell on to deaf ears.

As we were approaching the Police Station we encountered a policeman accompanied by a big, fat, burly civilian who called out 'Who have you there?' Unfortunately, the guard replied 'A *flieger*'. To the scream of '*Schweinhund*' the civilian threw a punch at the side of my jaw which, fortunately, I just managed to ride. This was followed by a blow to the other side which, again, I rode. Even so, I began to wonder what next to expect.

Curses rained down over my head and I had distinct visions of being hung from the nearest lamp post. Fortunately, however, the guard led me into the safety of the Police Station.

After being searched I was put into a cell and, seeing a flask of water, walked towards it. But the guard was there first, snatched it from beneath my nose and informed the policeman that food and water were strictly forbidden. No doubt that was punishment for my saying the overalls had been purchased from a German guard.

Sometime during the night the shift must have changed because another policeman entered the cell and on wakening I asked if I might have some water. He appeared to be quite astounded that the flask had been removed from the cell and he escorted me to the washroom. Also he produced another flask which I was allowed to fill before returning to the cell.

The following morning I was collected by the Army and felt quite honoured that I warranted two guards. Possibly, being aircrew and an escaped PoW, I may have been considered too dangerous for a single guard.

Needless to say, there no was no question of either breakfast or rations for the journey. On the other hand, as rations were usually issued at mid-day and in the afternoon it would be a case of waiting until I arrived at my destination.

We marched to the railway station where, after a short wait, we boarded a passenger train. I went to enter a compartment but was ordered to stand in the corridor. Apparently that morning only Germans were permitted to be seated. As it so happened it was a short journey so standing was not a problem.

We alighted at Torgau and, as we marched through the town, I thought how nice it was, especially with the river running through. The water looked cool and inviting but that only made me feel even more thirsty and hotter. One consolation was that we were ignored, completely, by the passers by.

Our destination proved to be Stalag IVD, where, after being handed over to the Camp Authorities, my particulars were taken yet again. I repeated the information given to the Feldwebel at Elsterwerda, and I was accepted as John Richmond.

For some reason unknown I was not searched but was led, immediately, to one of the downstairs cells. Shortly afterwards I was joined by a soldier, in British Army battle dress, who introduced himself as being Palestinian and that he had just finished fatigues – cleaning windows. Although he said he was serving a sentence he did not divulge his crime. However he was in possession of a Red Cross food parcel and, very decently, gave me food and several cigarettes.

As in one corner of the cell there was a bucket of water, I took the opportunity of having a strip down wash, after which my spirits improved immensely.

We spent the afternoon talking and he asked me numerous questions about England and especially about the girls in Nottingham.

Unfortunately, the cell had only one bunk and during the night I was awakened by his advances, to which I objected most strongly. However, later in the night, he made further advances and I had no hesitation in taking him by the scruff of the neck and leaving him very much the worse for wear.

The following morning, much to my relief, I was escorted from the cell and joined a party of some thirty other PoWs upstairs. They were a mixture of French, Italian and Russian plus a solitary American.

As the roll was called I nearly blew my cover as when I heard the name 'Rickmond' I did not respond and only when it was repeated did I realise that 'Rickmond' was the German pronunciation of 'Richmond'. Fortunately, the incident passed over without any repercussions.

With the Roll Call completed and the unteroffizier satisfied that the party was all present and correct we were marched out of the Camp and back to Torgau railway station. When the train drew in we were ushered into reserved compartments and as conversation was not '*verboten*', I spoke to the American and discovered his name was Phillips and that he was Army and not Air Force.

We changed trains at Falkenberg, from where we caught the train to Mühlberg for the march back to Stalag IVB and arriving about midday.

Arriving back at the Camp we were formed up in the Vorlager for the inevitable recount and satisfied that he had not lost any of his charges the guard entered the Guard Room. Whilst he was inside I spotted a British Army Sergeant and, calling him over, handed him my food and overalls with a request that he would pass them on to a friend of mine, named Joe, and gave him the hut number.

The guard reappeared from the Guard Room, and we were marched to the Delousing Compound. Whilst there I asked one of South African attendants to get a message to Joe requesting a change of clothing. The return message was that he would endeavour to spring me from the Straffe Compound prior to being put in to Solitary.

Naturally I was not enamoured by his proposal as I would have thought it easier to effect a substitution in the Delousing Compound than in Straffe where the security would be far tighter. However, the matter was out of my hands.

Whilst we were waiting to enter the showers, a gleam of hope appeared in the form of two RAF Sergeants, complete with blankets and kit, who were destined for a spell in Sick Quarters.

My immediate thoughts were that if two PoWs had entered the Delousing Compound it was conceivable that three PoWs leaving might escape notice. I explained my hastily formed plan to them and they agreed to cooperate.

Fortunately, in addition to underpants, I was wearing a pair of khaki shorts beneath my trousers so that when our clothes reappeared I hurriedly dressed, omitting the trousers and shirt. Borrowing a blanket from one of the Sergeants, I rolled up the trousers, shirt and blanket into a respectable bundle.

The first hurdle was over but the real test was yet to come. As soon as one of the Sergeants was dressed I said, 'Come on' and we walked out of the rear of the building. As we came to the front of the building and turned to leave the Compound we passed the guard from Torgau, the South African attendants and the German personnel in charge of the Compound.

With bated breath we walked through the open gateway and on to road to the Vorlager. The road was some 200 yards long, absolutely straight and did not afford any cover.

We had reached the halfway stage when we heard the Germans calling and, whilst my companion returned to the Compound, I continued slowly onwards. When he rejoined me, he explained that the Germans had thought we were walking rather quickly for Hospital cases but they had been satisfied with his explanation.

As soon as we had reached the Vorlager and turned to the right into the main camp, I returned the blanket, expressed my gratitude and took to my heels, dodging between the huts until I reached Joe's abode.

Once he had recovered from his initial surprise I recounted the story of the escape and re-capture, stressing that no cover had been provided at Point 'B'. I did not say how I had escaped from the De-lousing Compound.

A Red Cross food parcel was arranged, and I was informed that as a Sergeant Shaw had escaped that morning, it would be convenient if I became his cover. Naturally I had no objections to this arrangement.

Having reported to the Barrack Chief, in Hut 36B, and explaining I was Sgt. Shaw's cover and that it was essential that I should not be discovered, I was shown the whereabouts of my bunk and after depositing my few belongings I went in search of Ginger Dixon.

Chapter 20

Undercover

Later that afternoon when I was with Joe, Henri arrived and expressed his surprise at seeing me. I explained my complete dissatisfaction with cover not being provided at Point 'B' and should there be a next time with the misfortune of being recaptured whilst in limbo at Elsterwerda then, on my return to Stalag IVB, he would be for the high jump. In no uncertain terms I intimated that nothing would give me greater pleasure than giving him a sound thrashing.

The evening Roll Call passed without incident even though I had taken the precaution of positioning myself in the middle of the back row. With Roll Call being held indoors and with the lighting not being particularly brilliant, the chances of being recognised by the Duty Unteroffizier were somewhat lessened.

However at ten o'clock, the door opened and in strode the unteroffizier to the cries of 'Appel'. Although we were counted and recounted and each time the tally was correct, the unteroffizier was not satisfied and resorted to a name Roll Call.

Again the tally was correct but again he was not satisfied and repeated the Roll Call with each PoW kneeling on the floor as he answered his name. To his surprise, but not to ours, everyone was on the floor and no names were left on the list. At this point he acknowledged defeat by dismissing us and, together with his stooge, departed from the hut.

Immediately, I searched for the Barrack Chief and obtained Shaw's PoW and RAF identity numbers. The incident had been too close for comfort and if there was to be a recurrence, then I wanted to be forearmed. It was galling to be told that if there had been an identity problem it was a pre-arranged procedure for there to be a convenient lighting failure to allow sufficient time for the person concerned to disappear. It would have been far less traumatic to have been informed of the arrangement before and not after the event.

Having decided to turn in for the night, from across the gang-way it was impossible not to overhear someone recounting to his neighbour that, earlier in the day, a re-captured British PoW, whilst in the De-lousing Compound, had slipped his guard and that no one knew how it had been achieved. Apparently the PoW had disappeared into thin air and although the building was subjected to a thorough search, no trace of him could be found. Although I could have enlightened them I merely closed my eyes and, with a quiet smile on my face, went to sleep.

The following morning we were awakened by frenzied activity outside in the Compound. Looking through the windows we could see SS troops and members of the Gestapo milling around. In addition it appeared that each of the huts was under guard and we were soon to discover that we were under lock and key.

We watched as Sections 'A' and 'B' of huts 43 and 45 were evacuated and the occupants, complete with kit, were assembled. Each PoW was subjected to a photographic check followed by a body and kit search. Later, we learned that the huts were turned inside out.

We expected that once the searches had been completed, if that for which they had been searching did not come to light, they would move into huts 34 and 36.

As we did not see anyone being led away then who ever was 'wanted' was not found. Whether anything was found no one had any idea. But as quickly as they arrived, the SS and Gestapo departed.

It is at this point that the logic of the German Authorities becomes a mystery. With a photographic check being effected and drawing a blank, why did they not repeat the procedure with huts 34 and 36? Surely they must have realised that if they returned, whoever they were seeking would have been spirited away. Similarly, any contraband would be found an alternative hiding place.

With their departure life returned almost to normal except that whilst having the freedom of the Compound, the gates were locked and guards were stationed either side of the gates.

The thought of a possible return visit was not at all appealing as there was no way that a photographic check could be hoodwinked. Virtually anywhere would be better than the RAF Compound. My decision to leave was discussed with the Barrack Chief and an escape plan was evolved. During the afternoon a small crowd gathered between hut 45 and 43; others were kicking a ball around between the latrine and the 'danger' wire and look outs were positioned at strategic points. The makings of the necessary diversions, should they be required, were in place.

Positioning myself at the rear of hut 34 and lying immediately parallel to the fence, I waited for the signal that the Compound guard was out of sight and that the Gate guard had his back towards me. Using a piece of blanket to deaden any possible sound I cut through the inner wire and crawled into the space between the fences. Once safely inside I crawled up to the intersecting double fence which was the most dangerous part of the operation as, at this point, I came into view from the Perimeter Watch Tower.

Being given the signal that the Watch Tower guards had been distracted by the football crossing the 'danger' wire I cut through the near side wire, scrambled through and quickly cut the outer wire. When safely in the Army Compound I hooked the wire back into position, knowing that the inner wire in the RAF Compound would be, likewise, re-hooked.

Dusting myself down I walked across the compound to Joe's hut for a Council of War with the Escape Committee. It was suggested that I should move into the Army Compound below the RAF Compound but it would be necessary for me to obtain the agreement and co-operation of the Barrack Chief and also to make my own arrangements for avoiding Roll Call.

As it was necessary to hide somewhere and as Ginger Dixon was in that Compound, I agreed to the proposals – especially as it would be for only a short period whilst the necessary arrangements were made for a further outside excursion.

Before taking my departure, the Committee said they would arrange for my place, in hut 36B, to be taken and that later in the day I would be able to collect a Red Cross food parcel.

Ginger was in his hut and after putting him in the picture he introduced me to the Barrack Chief. It was agreed that I could stay in the hut and occupy one of the spare bunks. However, apart from arranging for Ginger's group to receive an increased ration, the Barrack Chief made it quite clear that I was on my own and if there was any trouble not to expect any assistance. I had no alternative but to agree to his terms.

I added that I did not foresee any problems emanating from the other PoWs as with being a friend of Ginger I was constantly in and out of the hut and used to being seen.

At the outset avoiding Roll Call was a straightforward exercise. Fortunately, there were several holes in the ceiling sufficiently large to crawl through and so, once the hut was empty, it was just a case of clambering on to a top bunk and hauling myself up into the roof space. When the whistle was blown signifying that Roll Call was over, it was the reverse procedure; nothing could be more simple.

The ceiling was asbestos pinned to the underside of the roof joists similar to current building practice, the only difference being that asbestos has been superseded with plaster board.

Roll Calls came and went without any problem until the morning of the third day. Hearing the dismissal whistle I started to edge my way back to the hole when, unfortunately, I missed my footing. The ceiling gave way and, amidst a cloud of dust, I disappeared through the hole much to the startled amazement of other PoWs re-entering the hut.

Fortunately, I landed on a top bunk because if I had fallen on the brick floor I could have sustained injuries. Without a word and covered in dust I brushed passed the onlookers and made a bee-line for the washroom. Unfortunately, the bunk on which I had landed was looking slightly worse for wear.

After that episode I decided that the roof space was not such a good spot and that an alternative hidey-hole had to be found. The only place which could be used, and which had been discounted previously, was beneath the bunks. By utilising several empty Red Cross boxes it was possible to arrange a 'hide' which should pass a cursory inspection.

During this period, daily contact was maintained with the Escape Committee Leader and, within a week, my name was back at the top of the list. Undoubtedly some leap-frogging had taken place but, possibly, it may have been thought my position was tenuous due to escaping from the De-lousing Compound. On the other hand it may have been the reward for my initiative.

Through the grapevine had filtered the news that the unfortunate guard had been sentenced to twenty-eight days detention for his misdemeanour.

I was introduced to an Army Staff Sergeant – 'Tish' Isherwood – who was to be my travelling companion. We were informed that the break was planned for 7.30 am the following morning and that we should be given further details later in the day.

With the break coming only eight days from my return to Stalag IVB there had not been sufficient time to build up a new stock of food but as my original stock was in the hands of the Contact at Point 'B', it was not too worrying. However, when Ginger and his pals proffered chocolate and cigarettes they were gratefully accepted and, at least, I would not be completely empty-handed.

Later that day, Tish and I were informed that the final briefing would be at 7 am the following morning, and that the escape would be through the wire. We were assured that the plan had been used previously and there was no necessity to have any worries. Even so, the news was nerve shattering but if, as had been said, it had been successful in the past then all we needed to do would be to implement instructions.

Fortunately, as the pre-briefing had been during the evening it was soon time to turn in for the night and there was not too much time to dwell on the prospect. Even so, it did not prevent the night being restless, especially with knowing that there must be no question of over-sleeping.

The following morning, after a quick wash and shave, I said my farewells to Ginger and reported for final briefing. Tish was waiting with the Escape Committee Leader and on my arrival we were informed that it was necessary to delay the escape for twenty-four hours and that we would be joined by two others. No reason was given for the delay nor were we given any intimation as to the identity of our new companions.

I, and presumably Tish, was left with a feeling of utter deflation after being keyed up for the escape. The first thing was to return to the hut in time to hide before Roll Call and, afterwards, to surprise Ginger with my still being around.

It was some time before the feeling of deflation disappeared and I could concentrate, fully, on whatever I was doing but, somehow or other, the day slowly passed.

The next day, with fingers crossed, I again reported for final briefing and it was with relief that I heard the escape would not be further delayed.

We were handed French Army jackets and overalls and then briefed. Afterwards we donned the overalls and jackets and made our way to the Vorlager where various work parties were being assembled.

We walked towards the Main Gate and turned left towards the Wood Compound, which was at the extreme end of the roadway.

Walking along the road we noticed that the perimeter fence was single and not the usual double lane. We passed two huts, on the left hand side, and just before we reached the Compound we about turned and retraced our steps. As we walked back we could see the farm wagon, which was used to collect wood, being pulled and pushed along by several Army personnel. As instructed, we walked behind one of the huts.

At this spot there was a slight bend in the roadway and the fence, and we had been briefed that because of the bend the field of vision from the Watch Towers, positioned at the Main Gate and the corner of the Wood Compound, was impaired.

From the Main Gate, the guards could see anyone walking inside the fence but beyond the bend they could not see whether you were inside or outside. Similarly the Corner guards could not see whether anyone was inside, or outside, until they had passed the bend.

As the wagon reached the bend, by sheer coincidence, one of the wheels fell off and whilst the Wood Party were struggling to replace it, one of them unhooked the previously cut wire and revealed a hole sufficiently large to clamber through both quickly and speedily.

The other two would-be escapees, who were following the wagon, walked between the wagon and the fence and stepped through the hole. Immediately being given the signal Tish and I followed suit, and the wire was re-hooked in readiness for the next escape.

As Tish and I walked along the outside road we realised the wheel had been replaced as we could hear the sound of the wagon, on the road, as it continued down to the Wood Compound.

This method of escape had been used previously and was to be used many times in the future. Its usage ended, eventually, due to the hole being discovered during a periodic inspection of the outer fence.

Chapter 21

A Second Taste of Freedom

Tish and I, plus the other two escapees, were on the outside and so far so good as it would appear that our escape had been effected unnoticed. It was only when we had rounded the bend that we realized how fortunate we were as a Party of Russian PoWs, under the watchful eye of a guard, were working in the field and within a hundred yards of the Camp. It would appear that, as with the Watch Tower guards, that guard also was unsighted as we slipped through the fence.

Without any undue signs of haste, we overhauled and fell into step with the other two PoWs and after turning the corner at the end of the fence and walking down the side of the Camp we could see the inmates leaving the huts in readiness for Roll Call.

It was difficult not to suppress a slight smile and the thought that they would have to cover for four missing PoWs did not occur to any one of us. It was to be much later that we were to learn that a pool of 'spare bodies' had been created by the simple expedient of reporting PoW's missing when, in point of fact, they were still within the confines of the Camp.

I understand that the 'pool' came to light only due to everyone being ordered into the Compounds and being counted whilst the huts were systematically searched. The net result was that over twenty missing PoWs were found.

As we walked down to Mühlberg we passed several groups of German soldiers on their way back to Camp. When we saw the first group we were apprehensive but when they, and succeeding groups, passed by we realized that, to them, we were just another working party on parole.

When we arrived at the Cemetery the usual French PoWs were already there and had started their various tasks. The Leader expressed his surprise at my being there but I quickly put him in the picture about the events of the previous ten days.

As I knew the position of the dug-out he said that he would escort our two companions and that Tish and I could follow later. This we did, crossing the field lower down and entering the wood from a different position. As we approached the dugout, we could see the Leader waiting to replace the brushwood over the entrance once we were safely below ground.

With four in the dug-out it was rather cramped but, at least, it was for that day only. There was the consolation that calls of nature would enable us to stretch out our legs.

We introduced ourselves and our new companions were Paul Manquet, RAF, and 'Mac' McClure, RCAF.

Tish was a regular soldier in the Honourable Company of the Royal Horse Artillery and made it quite clear that there was quite a distinction from the Royal Artillery and that the latter were accepted under sufferance. Over the days he regaled us with tales of Army life and, particularly, service in India. He had been captured in the North African desert and had arrived at Stalag IVB via a PoW Camp in Italy.

Paul had joined the RAF as a Boy Entrant and had trained as a 'ground' Wireless Operator. He was captured during the German invasion of Crete. His main complaint was that his brother had been declared medically unfit for the Armed services and had then promptly got his wife pregnant.

Mac, naturally, talked about life in Canada and extended an invitation for Paul to visit him after the war had ended. Strangely, when asked about the remainder of his crew he became very reticent and merely said that they were around somewhere. This did make Tish and

I think that, possibly, he had been shot down whilst on his inaugural 'second dicky' flight and did not wish the fact to be known.

I explained the details of my previous misfortunes and that I knew the route to Elsterwerda and the rendezvous. For this reason it was agreed that I should lead the way.

Paul produced a pack of cards and what better way to pass the time than indulging in a game. In answer to the inevitable question I admitted that although I could play Bridge, my knowledge was rudimentary and that I was not aware of any of the Conventions and that my bidding was very much a hit and miss affair. I did add that as I had played Whist for several years, playing the hand was not too difficult.

From the onset, it was Paul and Mac against Tish and myself. Tish was very patient, introducing me to Culbertson and also the intricacies and niceties of bidding. After each hand, time was spent in a constructive inquest.

The only time anyone left the dug-out was to answer a call of nature and making sure that the coast was clear. It was also the unwritten rule that whatever was necessary was done well away from the dug-out, not for just the obvious reason but also to ensure that if you had the misfortune to be caught in the act the others would remain undiscovered.

With three companions, and the added bonus of a pack of cards, the time passed away reasonably quickly and eventually the cards were put away due to the failing light. It was such a change from the previous occasion not to be continually looking at your watch to see the time.

As soon as dusk had given way to darkness we climbed out of the dug-out, replaced the brushwood cover and enjoyed the luxury of stretching our cramped limbs.

We walked to the edge of the wood and allowed our eyes to become accustomed to the darkness. As there was still a small amount of moonlight we decided to wait until it had disappeared below the horizon. However, as it was still in the sky at midnight we decided that if we waited any longer we would soon run out of travelling time. So, making sure that we could not see anyone, we jog-trotted across the potato field in order to reach my original starting point.

With the benefit of clear skies I took a bearing from Polaris and we struck off across country. Again taking repeated bearings to ensure we remained on course and, due to a certain amount of good fortune, we reached the canal within 50 yards of the bridge.

On the previous occasion, being on my own, I crossed over the bridge on my hands and knees. This time I could not allow the others to see that I was scared and so, nonchalantly, I stepped on to the bridge, silently uttered a prayer, and walked across. Once I had been joined by the others I did have the grace to admit to being scared and how I had previously crossed over the bridge. Whether or not to bolster my confidence, the others said they would have preferred to have crawled instead of walking.

As we walked through the first village it was almost as though the dog was awaiting my return as, immediately, he started barking. In the still of the night it was impossible to gauge how four pairs of Army boots, walking in step, must have sounded but, even with additional noise made by the dog, no one appeared to have been disturbed. On the other hand, if anyone had been awakened from their slumbers they had merely turned over and gone back to sleep.

Passing through the next village, one of the sleeping inhabitants objected, strongly, to being awakened from her slumbers as she opened the window and gave forth with a loud stream of invective. Naturally we chose to ignore her as we had no idea what she was saying, and we had no intention of offering our apologies for her rude awakening.

It was quite possible that in the darkness we could have been mistaken, quite easily, for four German soldiers and, who else, in the middle of the night, would have been walking in step?

As we reached the third village, dawn was beginning to break and so we made a slight detour. Shortly after regaining the road, workmen began to appear and we had to hurriedly take cover. It was obvious that it would be pushing our luck to continue much longer and that we had to find some suitable permanent cover.

After a short distance we spotted a small plantation which we were able to reach without being seen. However, once in the plantation it was not all that it had promised as the fir trees had been planted in rows and it was possible to see from end to end. Fortunately we were able to find one lane which had a slight dip in the middle and provided sufficient cover. Even so it was necessary to lie flat as the plantation was devoid of any undergrowth.

Making ourselves as comfortable as possible, we slept for the remainder of the morning, awakening to find, once again, the sun in the heavens. With some ten hours, or so, before us we spent the time playing talking in whispers and playing Bridge. Occasionally we would raise our heads to ensure that there was no likelihood of being discovered.

Dusk arrived and as daylight faded we were able to sit up and await the night. As soon as it was fully dark we were able to have a most welcome stretch. Fortunately, during the day, no one had suffered from either cramp or pins and needles and, also, we had been able to hold off calls of nature.

After waiting until midnight we continued the remaining short journey to Elsterwerda and passing, on the way, the small–holding which had been my previous hide but was, obviously, not suitable on this occasion. However on the outskirts of the town we were fortunate to find suitable cover on the top of a bank alongside the road. Even though there were houses on the opposite side we decided that we were sufficiently screened and we did have the added benefit of being able to sit up.

As on the previous day, we slept during the morning and spent the afternoon playing cards. With being so close to the road it was essential that movement, of any kind, and conversing, even in whispers, was restricted to the absolute minimum. Tish, unfortunately, would insist on having the occasional cigarette, which I thought was irresponsible as it was possible the smoke might have been seen and, also, it could have caused a fit of coughing. But of course, nothing untoward occurred and my protests appeared pointless.

At 7 pm, if we were to make our rendezvous, it was time to think about making a move. We crawled to the edge of the undergrowth and, making sure that all was clear, scrambled down the bank onto the road.

When we arrived at the level crossing the barrier was down and it was necessary to wait. Also at the crossing were a party of South African PoWs and although they stared quite intently, they either failed to recognize me or deliberately chose to turn a blind eye.

After only a short wait the train went by, the barrier was raised and we continued down the hill. As we came to the Russian Lager I noticed it was the same guard as previously that was on duty. Positioning myself so that I was screened from his field of vision, we were able to pass by without incident.

When we reached the garage the Contact was outside and, on seeing me, expressed surprise. After explaining what had happened I requested the return of my haversack and grub stake. He replied to the effect that as I had not returned that evening he surmised that I had been captured and so he had handed it to one of the later escapees. To me that sounded rather fishy and, undoubtedly, he had used the chocolate for his own nefarious purposes. It was obvious that no one would pass up a chance such as that.

I explained the situation to my companions and said that, in the circumstances, it would be better that we parted company and that I would continue on my own and live off the countryside. However the others, very graciously, would not agree to my suggestion and said that they would pool their resources with me.

We agreed to meet the Contact at midnight, but this time the precaution was taken not to entrust him with the food. As we returned to the track alongside the garage we spotted a small hollow, equivalent to a dried-up dew pond, complete with undergrowth. As we could not see anyone, we dived into the hollow and waited for midnight to arrive.

It was now a case of lying perfectly still, not talking and trying desperately not to cough or sneeze. Of course, Tish rather selfishly insisted on smoking even though the hollow was much too close to the track for comfort.

The four hours seemed to be interminable, and there was a quiet sigh of relief when darkness fell and even more so when it was midnight. All was quiet as we broke cover and waited near to the garage.

Out of the darkness appeared the Contact accompanied by a second Frenchman and we were guided, silently, down to the Marshalling Yard. Together with the second Frenchman we were instructed to wait in the undergrowth, at the side of the Yard, whilst the Contact looked for a suitable box-car.

When he re-appeared, he announced that he had found a box-car destined for Nancy, in France, and it appeared that we had struck lucky first time.

He led the way back to the box-car, wished us *'Bon Voyage'* and then departed, leaving the second Frenchman to open up the van and re-seal it once we were inside.

Although the Frenchman had no difficulty in removing the door seal undamaged, the door would not move. Close examination showed that the door was secured by a 1-inch-diameter bolt. As the Frenchman was without tools there was no option but to make good the seal and we returned to the side of the Yard whilst the Frenchman searched for an alternative box-car.

It was whilst waiting that I felt something crawling up my leg and, judging by their numbers, realized that they were ants and that must have been sitting on top of their nest.

Caution was thrown to the winds as I jumped up and down, twisting and turning in an attempt to rid myself of the wretched creature. The fact that there were German railway men in the yard was secondary to my discomfort. The battle was soon won, and I was able to return to my seat but ensuring that it was a few yards to one side.

In a short space of time the Frenchman reappeared with the news that he had been able to locate a box-car which carried a destination label inscribed 'Geneva'. This was indeed excellent news and a far better option than Nancy. We had immediate visions of the bright lights of neutral Switzerland and the possibility of a speedy return to England. At that time, we had not heard that Switzerland meant internment with the alternative of having trek through Occupied southern France and then Spain to Gibraltar before being repatriated.

But as quickly as we were given the morale boosting news, so the Marshalling Yard lights were extinguished, and we could hear the German railway men rushing here and there. As all shunting ceased abruptly, we decided that an Air Raid Alert must have been received and, silently, we cursed the RAF for their untimely interference.

We decided to wait to see what happened but after about fifteen minutes, as there did not appear to be any lessening of the commotion, the Frenchman said he thought it would be too dangerous for a group of five to attempt to cross the tracks. It was with great reluctance that we acquiesced to the logic of his argument that, even if we continued to wait, there was no guarantee that the trains would still be there when the Yard returned to normal.

Feeling very dispirited we agreed to abort the attempt and to return again the following evening. We retraced our steps to the garage and then decided to follow the track which ran alongside.

This led to a quarry which we circumnavigated and then entered the woods. Eventually we found an ideal spot in which to go to ground. This was a hollow with plenty of undergrowth and with the added advantage of there being a pond nearby.

After catching up on sleep we had the luxury of a wash in the pond and also a shave. The fact that it was cold water did not detract from the feeling of refreshment afterwards. Purely on the grounds of safety we took it in turns to visit the pond.

After the austereness of the three previous 'hides' the present one gave a feeling of luxury and although bitterly disappointed over the failure to leave Elsterwerda Marshalling Yard we became somewhat philosophical. Who knows, we might fare better tonight.

At midnight we returned to the rendezvous but drew a blank. In hindsight it appeared that, possibly, one of us should have returned to the garage at the usual time of eight o'clock but we had expected that the Frenchman would have informed the Contact of the aborted attempt.

We were left with no option but to return, feeling deflated and dejected, to our hide. During the night our fortunes most definitely took a turn for the worse as it started to rain.

Although at the beginning the rain was only light as the night progressed so did the intensity of the rain, finally culminating in a good, old fashioned thunderstorm. In no time at all we were soaked to the skin and as the temperature dropped so did our spirits and we were left feeling chilled to the bone and thoroughly miserable.

To ease our misery and discomfort we built a rough shelter out of brushwood and huddled together in an attempt to instill some warmth into our bones. For the first time since making our escape, the cards stayed in the box.

By late afternoon the rain was still coming down and we decided that enough was enough and roamed around the wood in the hope of finding more suitable shelter. At the edge of the wood we spotted what we thought was a Forest Warden's Look-out Tower and after ensuring that we were alone, ran across and climbed up the ladder. Inside did not appear to show any signs of recent usage and although the interior was small there was sufficient room to squeeze our bodies. Despite our discomfort, it was dry and that was more than enough to raise our spirits.

As warmth began to return to our bodies we talked over our prospects and came to the conclusion that one of us had to return to the garage, that evening, in the hope of meeting the Contact and arranging a rendezvous for midnight.

At half past seven, Tish moved off and, thoughtfully, took with him the water bottle and a packet of tea. Paul, Mac and I sat waiting and virtually counting the minutes before his return.

Two hours later Tish returned with the water bottle full of scalding hot tea which, initially, was passed around as a hot water bottle until the contents were cool enough to drink. The tea may have been without either sugar or milk but it tasted like sheer nectar as it warmed our stomachs. We had no hesitation in agreeing that it was one of the best, if not The Best cup of tea any one of us had drunk.

Tish explained that the Contact was surprised by his appearance as the other Frenchman had disappeared and he had assumed that we were en-route to Nancy. There was no doubt in our minds as to what had happened and that he had taken advantage of the general melee to board a truck and that it was he, and not us, that was on the way to somewhere. Whilst agreeing that it would have been difficult for five persons to avoid detection it would have been comparatively for a single person to have succeeded.

The first hour since Tish's return had sped by which meant that we had only one more hour to wait before leaving the Tower in order to make the midnight rendezvous. After being cramped together for the past six hours it was a delight to stretch our aching limbs.

The Contact was awaiting our arrival and we were led, once again, down to the Marshalling Yard where we waited whilst the Contact carried out a reconnaissance. When he returned he said the only sealed box-car was destined for Hindleveldt. Although it sounded Dutch we were not sure and certainly had no idea of its location. It could have been Dutch but on the other hand it could have been Flemish, but the last thing we wanted was the possibility of being in a train which might be strafed by Allied aircraft. So rather reluctantly we decided to forego the opportunity and wait until a known destination arose. If hindsight proved we had boobed, so be it.

As we returned to the Tower we came across a partly built house and, being inquisitive, decided to investigate. The ground floor and outside walls were completed but the ceilings and roof were missing so leaving it open to the elements.

Creeping around the ground floor we suddenly heard a clatter and the sounds of muffled cursing. The answer was soon apparent as it was Paul who had fallen down the steps leading to the basement. Fortunately, apart from possible bruises he had not suffered any injuries. Luckily the steps had walls either side because if one side had been open and Paul had fallen over the edge, with the floor being concrete, he could easily have broken either an arm or a leg.

As the floor was completely dry we decided that we should spend the night in the basement and managed a few hours of broken sleep. As daylight began to filter down into the basement and not knowing at what time the builders might start work it was obvious we could not remain there and so we returned to the safety of the Tower.

It was not long after being re-settled that we heard someone approaching and we froze. With the observation windows being closed it was impossible to see outside and it was a case of sweating it out. Unfortunately Tish had a sudden fit of coughing, no doubt due to too much smoking, and although he buried his head in his jacket, the noise was frightening and in the still of the early morning could not possibly escape the attention of anyone nearby.

But luck was on our side. Whoever it was moved away and we wondered if it was a fellow escapee who, on hearing the noise, thought the Tower was occupied by the Warden. On the other hand, all we had heard was the breaking of twigs, warning of an approach. It was conceivable that it could have been an animal, possibly a deer, and which had been scared off by the noise.

Whether human or animal we were not to know but we did decide that the Tower might not be such a good idea, at least during the day, and returned to our original 'hide'.

As the sun rose higher and higher the rise in temperature, following the storm of the previous evening, resulted in the air becoming humid. With being close to the pond it was not long before we were inundated with mosquitoes which were soon tucking into human flesh. All we could do was to swat continually in the vain hope of driving them away. When it came to shaving the mixture of cold water and facial bites made the operation somewhat painful.

During the morning as all was quiet we decided to have a walk but to remain within the confines of the wood. It was a relief to have a respite from the mosquitoes and being continually bitten. At the edge of the wood the heat from the sun slowly started to dry our clothes and at the same time our spirits were restored.

But like all good things the luxury of standing in the sunshine was not to last as in the distance we could hear the sound of Germans singing in unison. We did not wait to see who they were but, instead, scurried back like startled rabbits to the safety of the 'hide'. Although at first they appeared to be coming in our direction they veered away and we heard their voices disappearing into the distance.

Once again it was back to the old routine of passing away the time by playing cards. Under Tish's tuition and forbearance my bidding was improving but I still had a long way to go.

From time to time the cards would be put away and we would sit around talking over life both in the Services and Civvy Street and wondering what it would be like once the war was over and how life would compare with pre–war days.

Time slipped by and as the light began to fade we got our few things together to ensure that there would not be any trace of our having been there. We moved to the edge of the wood and waited until it was time to leave for our rendezvous.

Back at the garage we waited for the Contact to appear and then moved down to the Yard. As usual the Contact did the necessary scouting.

When he returned it was with the news that he had located a box-car destined for Hanover. Not exactly an ideal destination but it would take us westwards and from Hanover, or close by, we should be able to drop down into Holland.

For better, or worse, we agreed to take a chance. Each day which was spent at Elsterwerda was a drain on the food stocks which, in effect, had been reduced by a quarter by having me to feed.

We followed the Contact between the trucks, crossing several tracks before reaching the box-car. He removed the seal and opened the door, then once we were inside and we had confirmed that it was possible to open the window from inside, he re-closed the door and re-affixed the seal.

Another hurdle had been cleared and Elsterwerda would soon be left behind. We had no idea as to the contents of the box-car but, at that stage, all that concerned us was to make our selves as comfortable as possible and try to get some sleep.

That, temporarily, was completely out of the question as we were subjected to a certain amount of shunting and jolting as we hit the next truck. Eventually the shunting ceased, the train was complete and we slowly steamed into the night. After that sleep did not present a problem.

When we awoke, although we realized it was daylight outside it was gloomy inside due to only a small amount of light filtering through cracks in the wooden body.

As our eyes became accustomed to the gloom we realised that the box-car was loaded with furniture, no doubt belonging to a family moving to the West to ensure they were not overrun by the advancing Russian Armies.

Tish and Mac were luckier than Paul and I in as much that they were close to a mattress which they claimed as their domain. We were left to make ourselves as comfortable as possible wedged in the 'V' between large items of furniture. Not an ideal situation but bearable.

Although it was possible to open the windows, we decided that, as the boxcar was sealed it presented too much of a risk and so for ventilation and a certain amount of daylight we had to rely on being able to slide the door open about 2 inches.

It was just as well that we did not risk opening a window as we were to find that we were parked, in a siding, at Magdeburg which meant that we had travelled about 90 miles. The next question was how long would it be before we were moved. Knowing that Magdeburg had been bombed in the past, the thought of being parked there overnight was not at all appealing.

Inevitably the day was spent either playing cards or dozing. It was essential, however, that we maintained an aural look-out so that the door could be re-closed if we heard the sound of either voices or footsteps.

As it so happened we were parked only until nightfall so it would appear that freight trains ran at night only. No doubt the German Authorities thought they could defend trains that were in the Marshalling Yards whereas freight movement in daylight could be subjected to low level air attacks.

After nightfall, shunting re-commenced and after being moved around we were hooked up to a westbound train. We were left wondering where and how far from Magdeburg we would find ourselves at the next stop.

Those two questions were answered when we awoke the following morning. We had travelled a further 50 miles and were parked in a siding at Brunswick. In two nights since leaving Elsterwerda we had covered 125 miles, or thereabouts.

If we had been on foot and with the restricted hours of darkness we would have been lucky to have covered a quarter of the distance.

The only drawback that we could see to being in the box-car was that our water supply was running low and there was no way that it could be replenished. By the end of the day we would be without water and that meant that we would need to leave the train irrespective of whether it remained at Brunswick, stooped en-route or when it arrived at its next parking spot.

We knew that we were only some 35 miles from our final destination and it appeared unlikely that we would have a further daylight stop after leaving Brunswick.

But our supposition proved incorrect as the following morning found us parked at Lehrte and still 10 miles short of Hanover. If we were not moved into Hanover during the day we could drop off after dark. With only 10 miles to Hanover the box-car must be hooked up to a local freight train. Once in Hanover it could be unlocked for unloading onto a road vehicle. When that happened, unless we could hide in wardrobes, assuming there was sufficient free space to open the doors, then it would be curtains and we would be back in the bag.

By carefully opening a window either side we were able to take stock of our position. What we saw was not encouraging as on the one side, a few tracks away, stood a troop train whilst on the other side stood a flak train. Possibly this was the reason freight trains ran only at night especially if each of the main Yards was protected by its own flak train.

Our hope was that one, if not both, trains were moved as soon as it was dark. We, now, had to sit and sweat it out. Most definitely it was a case of will they or will they not.

Although we waited, patiently, for nightfall and then midnight before opening the windows we were greeted by the sight of both trains still in their sidings.

Being faced with Hobson's choice and almost a 'Heads you lose, Tails you lose' situation, one by one we clambered through the window and dropped to the ground. The last one out attempted to pull the window to in the hope that it would stay closed although even if it had been left open it is doubtful if it would have been noticed before daylight and possibly not until the box-car was either moved or opened.

Keeping in the shadows we crept towards the front of the train. The only reason we went towards the front of the train was that it appeared to be nearer that to the back.

After passing several box-cars the trucks were similar in design to cement or Saxa Salt wagons. The body frames were under-slung and provided insufficient clearance from the rails to allow anyone to crawl underneath.

Seeing a man approaching carrying a lantern which swung sideways as he walked, we dropped to the ground and huddled, as close as possible, to the rails. Unfortunately, we not alongside the couplings otherwise we could have darted between the wagons.

As he reached our position, the lantern swung in our direction and highlighted a body which, unfortunately, did not go unnoticed and he called out. Rather sheepishly Mac stood up, followed by Tish and Paul and finally by myself. Whether he would have seen me if I had not moved is pure conjecture, but it is just possible that he would have been satisfied with the three of them.

He was speechless, or almost as he managed to gasp, somewhat incredulously, 'One?', 'Two??', 'Three???', 'Four????' As he counted so did his bewilderment increase.

We were taken to a small office where he proudly showed his captives to his fellow workers. Their bewilderment was no less than his. One PoW was understandable, two PoWs it might have been acceptable but four PoWs were, most definitely, beyond their comprehension.

After establishing that we were English and in the Army with there being no possible question of being in the RAF they began a series of frantic telephone calls. It was obvious that there was nothing in the Rule Book which covered the recapture of four escaped PoWs. Eventually an Official, of sufficiently high authority, was contacted and peace of mind returned to our captors.

To the obvious relief of our captors, four armed guards arrived and took us into custody. Undoubtedly the story of our capture would be a talking point for several days to come.

Whilst being marched away I chatted to one of the guards and he freely admitted that the war was not good and that he hoped it end without too much more bloodshed. With tongue in cheek I asked about the Gestapo, but his lips were sealed.

Possibly he did not wish the others to know his thoughts because it was common knowledge that one word out of place and you could find yourself heading in the direction of the Eastern Front. And to the Germans that was their nightmare.

Arriving at the local Police Station we were searched and the food supply, watches, cigarettes etc. were confiscated. For what it may be eventually worth we were each handed a receipt in exchange. That night was spent two to a cell, Paul and Mac and Tish and myself.

The following morning our goods were returned and it was inevitable that about one third of the food and cigarettes were missing. Despite all our protestations the Policemen had the perfect answer. During the night the shift had changed and they were unaware that anything was missing. And you cannot argue against that.

We were handed over to two Army guards who escorted us, firstly, to Hanover where it was plain to see how it had suffered as the result of Allied bombing. From Hanover it was a further short journey to Fallingbostel and Stalag XIB which was to be our home for the next few weeks.

Chapter 22

Stalag XIB

After being searched we were housed in the Compound adjacent to the Straffe Compound and in which we recognized some former inmates of Stalag IVB. In point of fact, in talking to them it transpired that two of them were at Elsterwerda at the time of my first recapture. Although they had been told that a British PoW had been recaptured they were unaware of his identity. After saying that I was the PoW in question, and the circumstances of my recapture and subsequent second escape, I was assured that my grub stake was not handed to them nor, as far as they were aware, to any of the others who were at Elsterwerda at that time. This information confirmed my suspicions that the food had been purloined by the Contact.

When we received a delivery of Red Cross food parcels, we were told the Camp was occupied by British Army PoWs and we had visions of remaining at Stalag XIB after we had been released from Straffe.

A few days later, when we were visited by the Camp Leader from Stalag XIA, we learned that a number of the Army in XIA had been transferred from Stalag IVB. Knowing that we had escaped from IVB, the Camp Leader promised to enquire if we were known by any of the PoWs. His promise resulted in my receiving a letter from Ginger Dixon that was smuggled into Straffe with the delivery of the daily rations.

Eventually we were moved into the Straffe Compound and found the other occupants were members of the French Army. It appeared that they were guilty of various crimes, committed whilst PoWs, and were awaiting sentence.

Unlike previous accommodation, the hut was equipped with double tier bunks but, apart from that difference, the furnishings were standard pattern.

Although the hut was only a few yards from the perimeter fence, the only means of escape would have been by tunnel.

This was discounted on two counts, the first being we had no idea how long we would be in residence and the second being we would require the full co-operation of the other PoWs.

The days of waiting became more tedious as each day passed. Although we were able to walk round the small compound which provided a measure of exercise, the novelty soon began to pall. Even playing cards seemed boring and I attributed the ennui as being the effect of the anti-climax of two escapes interspaced with the excitement and tension of living under cover. But, by degrees, the ennui disappeared and we became more relaxed.

One morning, in early September, we were awakened by the sound of church bells and later, through the grapevine, we heard that the Allied Armies had attempted to secure a bridgehead over the Rhine by Airborne Landings at Arnhem. Our spirits soared because the Rhine crossing would open up the way into north-west Germany and resulting, possibly, in our early release from captivity.

Within a few days our hopes were dashed by the sight of a bedraggled column of Red Beret troops being marched into the Camp. History has shown how a gallant attempt to secure the bridgehead resulted in abject failure and severe loss of life.

It was possible, when collecting the daily rations, to talk to some of them and hear of their ordeal. But the guards intervened and terminated any conversation.

One day we saw one of their number caught in the act of stealing a few potatoes whilst collecting rations. In a PoW Camp, stealing from your compatriots was considered to be the most serious of crimes. Punishment would be swiftly administered and entailed the convicted

PoW being straddled across a table, his trousers pulled down to the ankles and then to receive he specified number of lashes from an Army issue leather belt. As one would expect, the PoW did not repeat the crime and it was a deterrent to others.

As a variation from Bridge, from time to time we would indulge in Double Patience, using two packs of cards. Another form of Patience, the name of which we were unable to discover, was to place the cards face upwards. If the outer of three successive cards were either the same suit or face value, the third card would be placed over the second card. As the game progressed and single cards became multiples then the cards beneath the 'same' card would be moved. The object was to finish with two stacks only. This we found most infuriating as no one succeeded in ending with two stacks.

I discovered that one of the regular guards spoke quite good English due to, pre-war, serving on the German Atlantic liners. One evening he told me that he was due to go home on leave and would I exchange some chocolate for a loaf of bread? I had no hesitation in agreeing to his proposal and a 'price' was fixed.

However, the following evening he produced only part of a loaf and it would appear that he was denying himself his daily ration so that he could take home some chocolate as a treat for his wife and children. It was necessary to make it quite clear to him that the chocolate would be handed over only when we had received a complete loaf.

Unfortunately for him, the day before he was due to make his final delivery we were moved out. There was no way that we could get the chocolate to him because the introduction of a third person would undoubtedly have resulted in the chocolate being retained by that third person.

We had been in Straffe for six weeks which, as it so happens, could have given sufficient time to have tunneled our way out. At a rate of 3 feet each day we would have been well clear of the perimeter fence. But hindsight is that which you do not have at the outset.

We were accompanied by two guards who treated us quite courteously and, in return, we gave them cigarettes. At Hanover, as there was a lengthy delay before the connecting train was due to depart, we were taken into the city and shown the main church and a number of historic buildings which had escaped damage during various air raids.

Whilst sitting in one of the parks, there was a mother and young boy about three years of age. A lovely little boy with blonde curly hair and a skin that was almost translucent. When we offered him some squares of chocolate his eyes lit up with sheer delight. Sharing his joy helped to ease our conscience over the misfortune of the guard back in Stalag XIB.

But as it always happens time ran out and we were escorted back to the railway station and eventually we arrived, late evening, at Mühlberg. As it was dark with an overcast sky and no moon, Paul did say that if I had any thoughts of making a break would I leave the food behind? But it was almost the end of October and without an overcoat there was no way that I could have survived the oncoming cold, and most probably wet, weather. Needless to say, if I had have made a run for it then most certainly I would not have left the food behind.

For the first time, seeing the lights of Stalag IVB almost made them seem welcome.

Chapter 23

In Straffe at IVB

Once again I was back in Stalag IVB and wondering what the future might have in store. After being booked in at the Guard Room our friendly guards were dismissed and we were put in the cells. No doubt the inquisition would commence the following morning.

However with the dawn of a new day the expected did not occur. We were subjected to the mandatory de-lousing and since my previous return it would appear that security had been tightened as we were counted both entering and leaving the showers and again once our clothes had been returned and we were dressed.

With such an eagle eye there was no opportunity to quietly disappear into thin air. Even without the repeated counting it would not have been possible to do a disappearing act as we were the sole occupants and consequently there was no one with whom one could mix.

After ensuring yet again that we were still a squad of four we were marched, unceremoniously, to the Straffe Compound to await interrogation prior to being sentenced to solitary confinement.

The American, Phillips, who was in the Party when I returned from Stalage IVD, two months previously, was still in residence.

Also I renewed acquaintance with Private Blueitt who had been Joe's sidekick. From him I learned that my Chess friend had been shot and killed whilst scaling the Straffe Compound fence. Apparently he had made practice of scaling the fence after evening roll call, and spending the night with friends in the Camp, before returning early the following morning.

Unfortunately one morning he was spotted by the guards climbing down the fence and it was a case of shoot first and ask questions afterwards.

The hut was occupied by a mixture of British, the lone American, French and Russians. As Tish held the senior British rank it was agreed, mutually, that he would assume the position of British Leader.

By general agreement the British, American and French occupied one half of the hut with the Russians at the other end. It was definitely a case of West is West, East is East and ne'er the twain shall meet.

During the first morning we each received a Red Cross food parcel and we gathered from the other British PoWs that parcels were issued on a weekly basis. At least we were not going to be short of either food or cigarettes.

One morning one of the British PoWs awakened early due to a call of nature and on his return from the latrine he realised that his food parcel was missing. The alarm was raised and it was quickly established that other parcels, also, were missing. A systematic search was carried out and it was established that some of the Russian PoWs were the perpetrators and, to our disgust, the tinned food had been thrown into the latrine.

One of the Russians dashed out into the Compound with me close on his heels. He took refuge behind the guard who held me at arms length with the point of his bayonet. However once I had explained what had happened the Russian was handed over immediately.

Back in the hut no time was lost in determining which of the Russians were involved and each, in turn, was systematically thrashed. Their Leader made no protest at the punishment.

The question of the stolen food was discussed with the Camp Leader – Myers, RCAF and ex-Stalag Luft VI – who, to our utter disgust, refused to make any recompense.

Some days later we were awakened to a strange sight. During the previous day the adjoining Compound had been evacuated and the new occupants were in residence – Polish women prisoners.

Although not allowed to speak to them we were able to throw packets of cigarettes over the wire. Later in the day we were horrified to find Phillips trying to scrounge cigarettes from them.

A new inmate arrived, RAF, and complete with Argentine Red Cross food. Unhesitatingly Phillips sat beside him and remarked that he had not seen any Argentine food. The RAF Sergeant accepted the bait and invited Phillips to try some. In a single movement, Phillips drew a jack knife from his pocket, opened the blade whilst the knife was in motion and within a couple of seconds was vigorously buttering biscuits. Greased lightning would have taken second place.

With the knowledge that sooner or later we would be subjected to interrogation we decided on the story that was to be told and which was rehearsed until we were word perfect.

My version was that I had escaped at the end of August by cutting through the wire opposite to Hut 22 and which was in the Army Compound adjacent to the RAF Compound. At the time it did not occur to us that the Germans might check that length of fence for signs of a break-out. Once outside I had headed north and some ten days later, on the outskirts of Falkenberg, I had met the others. Believing them to be French, due to their clothing, I had spoken to them and was surprised to find that my surmise was incorrect and, in fact, they were fellow Englishmen. Or to be strictly correct, two English and one Canadian. By sheer coincidence they had also escaped from Stalag IVB and so we decided to join forces.

The Interrogator appeared to be satisfied with the explanation and, when all said and done, it was plausible. When asked how we had travelled to Lehrte, I replied that we had waited at an overbridge until a slow moving freight train, with open wagons, passed underneath and we dropped down. I added that, fortunately, none of us was injured by the fall. Naturally in order to escape detection the overbridge was away from the town and the drop was made during darkness.

Although subjected to cross questioning on various points I was able to answer without any difficulty or hesitation.

With the interrogation complete I was dismissed and escorted back to the Straffe Compound.

As we were not subjected to any further interrogation it would appear that our stories tallied, for which we were truly thankful. If there had been too much questioning it is possible that one of us may have inadvertently made a slip.

The days of waiting passed slowly by as walking was extremely limited. We did not have any books to read and as I was the sole Chess player we were left to either Bridge or Patience. Even conversation became desultory.

We were surprised by the appearance of Henri, the Frenchman who had run the Camp end of the escape route. Apparently he had been caught indulging in Black Market activities, no doubt using as currency some of the cigarettes handed over by the Escape Committee.

We learned from him that the Elsterwerda Contact was in prison as the result of being picked up by the Gestapo. Not, as we thought, for his involvement in the escape route but due entirely to his relationships with German women.

A Dutch arrival confirmed that Hindleveldt was in south-west Holland. Naturally we kicked ourselves, mentally, for not having the courage to have taken a chance with the box-car at Elsterwerda.

In all, six weeks were spent in the Straffe Compound and to our complete amazement we bypassed Solitary Confinement and were released into the Camp. Possibly the Authorities had decided that the time spent in Straffe plus the time at Stalag XIB was sufficient punishment for our escape.

Chapter 24

A Change of Identity

Having reported to the Camp Leader we were allocated new quarters and having introduced ourselves to the Barrack Chief we sorted out four empty bunks. Apparently the hut was occupied by bad guys, very few of whom had changed their ways, and so we would be in good company.

The first few days were spent in enjoying the luxury of the freedom within the camp and looking up old acquaintances. All of them were surprised to see us and had been convinced that as we had been 'missing' for such a long time we had succeeded in making a 'home run'.

Although Red Cross food parcels were still available, the issue had been reduced to one parcel between two persons. However, with being a foursome we were able to store a small amount of food, each week, towards Christmas which was only two weeks away.

Christmas was spent as the previous one in 1943 but I think that in 1944 our spirits had sunk a little lower. Although the nightly BBC news spoke of progress on both the Western and Eastern Fronts it seemed to be painfully slow. Certainly, the Germans were contesting every inch of the Homeland.

After Christmas Paul was taken ill, but although necessitating two weeks in Hospital it was not as serious as at first thought and we were pleased to have him back.

We were shocked by the Ardennes Push and, in particular, the speed of the German advance. We were even more disheartened by the arrival of the American 106th Division which had been captured just two days after being thrust into the Front Line. If that was not bad enough we discovered that a week previously they were in New York.

Fortunately, the American Sector was strengthened by the arrival of British forces and coupled with the German push running out of steam the advance was halted and the Front stabilized.

In order to accommodate the Americans each hut had to accept 100 extra PoWs which meant sleeping three to two bunks.

To make matters worse, the sudden influx of PoWs exhausted the stock of Red Cross food parcels and we were back to the basic rations. In the middle of winter that was the last thing we wanted to happen.

As light relief, one morning in the Washroom was an American wearing his greatcoat with the collar turned up and attempting to have a wash. What appeared even more humorous was another American with a tablet of soap which floated and was delighted that to pick up the soap he needed only to put his finger tips into the cold water.

As the days passed the Americans were gradually thinned out as they were transferred to other Camps and it was no small relief to have a bunk to oneself.

One afternoon there was a mild sensation in the Camp with the sight of Swiss Red Cross lorries arriving. There was no shortage of volunteers to assist in unloading although one volunteer was caught trying to purloin some of the contents of an opened parcel. Unfortunately, the delivery was sufficient only for an issue of one parcel between ten PoWs, but even that was better than nothing.

As January gave way to February, I began to get restless and the feeling was not helped by the thought of possibly being released by the Russian Army. So having discussed my ideas with Tish and although he thought my idea of a further escape at this late stage of the War to be somewhat stupid, it was agreed that I should leave the combine.

After discussions with Joe, I was passed over to the Escape Committee Leader and he agreed to my idea of trying to join one of the small Kommandos that were still leaving the Camp.

During my waiting time, Dresden was subjected to a night and day of merciless bombing. The city was filled with refugees fleeing from the advancing Russian Armies and the night raid by the RAF was followed, in daylight, by the USAAF. There has been more than enough comment and controversy on those two raids without adding my own thoughts.

At last, I was able to make contact with a Paratrooper – Private Robert Leighton from 8 Barrack Street, Carlisle – who was willing to exchange identities. His reason for not wanting to go out on Kommando was because it would mean leaving his pals. Fortunately he was in the next hut and so it was a simple matter to swap places. All I now had to do was to sit and wait in the hope that the Kommando left the Camp without the switch being noticed.

Fortunately, the wait was not long as the following morning we were paraded, names called and marched up to the De-lousing Compound. Unfortunately after de-lousing the Kommando was cancelled and we returned to the hut. The only consolation, for me, was that I had had the benefit of a hot shower.

Rather disconsolately I resumed my original identity. But it was to be for forty-eight hours only as two days later, at 5.30 am, I was awakened by Robert with the news that the Kommando was back on and did I still want to go.

There was no question of my not going and I hurriedly dressed and threw my belongings into my kit-bag. As I dashed down to the latrine I passed one of my acquaintances who, surprised at seeing me fully dressed, asked where I was going. Grinning from ear to ear I replied that after a quick loo I was going home. The reply he gave was only to be expected in as much he told me not to be such a stupid so and so.

It was now a case of getting into the next hut. Obviously if Robert had made it then I should be able to make it in the reverse direction. From the Washroom window it was possible to see the guard as he walked back and forth across the front of the huts and determine the time interval between appearances.

The next time the guard disappeared from view I dropped out of the window, accepted my kit-bag from Robert, sprinted across the gap, threw my bag through the open window and dived head-first after it, ably assisted by Robert's pals who were waiting for me.

I had barely sufficient time to regain my breath before the Kommando was called on Parade, counted and marched out of the Compound.

As we had been de-loused two days previously it was deemed unnecessary to be de-loused again and we were halted outside the Search Barrack. In checking my belongings I was asked to account for my blanket and, quite truthfully, I replied that it was in a parcel that I had received from my mother. Fortunately he did not consider it strange that Robert Leighton had received a parcel, from home, in the short space of time that he had been in Stalag IVB or, for that matter, in captivity.

My heart went into my mouth when I realized that we were to be subjected to a photographic check because, apart from height and build, Robert and I bore no resemblance to one another. But Lady Luck was with me as I was passed through and joined the others waiting outside.

After yet another inevitable count we were marched out through the Main Gate, turning left to march down to Mühlberg railway station. Having been down to Mühlberg on numerous occasions I think I could have made it blindfolded.

We caught a train up to Falkenberg and then whilst waiting for a connection we were issued with rations. Although I spoke to the guards it was not possible to establish our destination. Even if I had have been told, without a map I would have been none the wiser.

When the train arrived, we were shepherded inside and ordered to stand in the corridor due to all the seats being Occupied. The train pulled out of the station and almost immediately swung westwards over the points.

A lady passenger passed me some food and in quite good English explained that she had a son in Manchester. However, our conversation, as usual, was curtailed by one of the guards making it quite clear the talking was strictly '*verboten*'.

The train stopped short of Halle and we were ordered to jump down onto the ground. After being counted and satisfied we were all present and correct we were marched towards and through Halle to the western side. It was evident that the Halle had been subjected to Allied bombing and was in a sorry state.

As we were marched up a hill all the buildings, with the exception of the Hospital which was situated at the top, had been hit. How it had escaped being hit was either a miracle or the result of some high precision daylight bombing.

From our uniform it was obvious that we were British and we were subjected to screamed invective from a woman passerby. I hate to think what may have been the outcome had she known I was in the RAF. Strangely enough the guards turned their rifles towards her and she stopped screaming and moved away.

When we reached the railway and were told to halt we realized that Halle railway station must be out of use and that it was here that we would get the next train.

This time we were not aware as to which direction we were travelling but, after stopping at several wayside stations, we arrived at our destination which turned out to be Wallwitz, situated between Halle and Berlin.

By this time, darkness had fallen and after marching through the village we arrived at what appeared to be a converted Church Hall or similar. The windows were barred horizontally and vertically but it looked as though there could be sufficient space through which it might be possible to squeeze your head.

I had heard the tale that if your head would go through the space between bars then your body would follow. The reasoning behind the theory is that the skull is the only part of the body which cannot compress whereas the torso, arms and legs can be contorted, virtually, into any shape.

The following morning, we sorted ourselves out and I teamed up with two Paratroopers. I made no bones about my intention to escape and to travel cross country, in a westerly direction, until I made contact with the Allied Forces. Both Paratroopers agreed to take part in my escape bid.

That night I was able to put the bars theory to the test. Having got my head through the bars I found that it was possible, with a little difficulty, to squeeze through the gap. After collecting a few carrots from the garden I returned from whence I had come. The way out was now established and all that remained was to amass a small food stock.

The Kommando was split into two parties working on alternate days. The work consisted of tamping ballast between the railway line sleepers and the track bed. The amount of work actually completed was almost negligible, certainly not arduous, but what was achieved appeared to satisfy the guards.

As an added variation to our diet, on a working day we would take the opportunity to collect dandelion leaves which are a good substitute for 'greens'.

But both working and dandelion leaf collecting was short lived as the following week we were strafed by American Mustangs. Fortunately we managed to scramble down the embankment and no injuries were sustained. Needless to say we went on strike and, fortunately, the guards did not make any protest as they were also vulnerable.

On the Saturday evening we were allowed to walk outside the building and on the Sunday our freedom was extended to the whole of the village.

Finding a farm we watched the cows being milked and when we were offered some before it had been chilled we did not refuse. It was the first time I had had fresh milk since being shot down and it tasted absolutely delicious. What was even better was being given a meal of bacon and scrambled eggs.

Chapter 25

Homeward Bound

On the Monday morning we awakened to discover that, during the night, the guards had disappeared and we realised that we were free. When captured the Germans always announced that the war for you is over; now for us imprisonment was over.

Once the impact of freedom had well and truly sunk into our minds we hurriedly packed our belongings and returned to the farm where we were able to trade blankets for eggs and bread. We were now equipped for the first stage of the long trek homewards.

The walking part of the trip was comparatively short lived as during the afternoon we made contact with an American advance party. Once they realized that we were British and ex-PoWs they gave us cigarettes and 'K' rations.

Shortly after the Americans continued eastwards we flagged down a Jeep returning from Halle. As there were only three of us we were able to hitch a lift and a couple of hours later we were dropped in a small village occupied by the Americans.

Intuition soon led us to the cookhouse where, after a hot meal, we stocked up with further 'K' rations and a small amount of tinned food.

Wandering round the village we found a Tobacconist's shop and as the owner had fled in advance of the arrival of the American Army, we had no compunction in indulging in a spot of minor looting and helped ourselves to boxes of cigars.

With no shortage of American movement, both eastwards and westwards, there was no problem in hitching lifts further west. In the evening, we had arrived at Teutschental and, deciding that was enough for one day, we succeeded in finding a billet in a private house.

We gave the housewife some eggs and asked if she would cook them for our supper. We sat talking and positively drooling at the vision of a plate of fried eggs. But it was not to be as we were served with flat, un-appetising looking omelettes.

Even though sleeping three to a bed, slipping between clean sheets was luxurious and after the excitement of the day it was not long before we were sound asleep. The following morning, on the other side of the village we found a British Kommando which was being used as a Staging Post for returning PoWs.

We added our names to the list of ex-PoWs and after being told that there was no chance of sufficient transport being available that day it was agreed that we could return to the village, but must report the following morning.

Borrowing bicycles, we cycled back to the village and arranged a 'new' billet with Frau Edith Saalfelt, Kurfurten Strasse 25. As it was opposite to our billet of the previous night it was easy to move our kit.

Naturally we made a bee-line for the American cookhouse and had a meal. Whilst there a GI handed us a chicken which, obviously, he had purloined from somewhere and an officer gave us three pheasants that he had shot earlier that morning.

Visiting the local bakery and indulging in a spot of bartering with cigars we were able to arrange for the birds to be roasted and also obtained two loaves of bread.

After collecting the roasted birds, on the way back to the billet we stooped off at the local inn and managed to obtain a pitcher of beer.

Armed with our spoils we returned to the billet, handed them over to Frau Saalfelt and invited the family to supper. The family, in addition to Frau Edith, included her mother and father together with her sister and baby daughter.

Frau Edith's husband was reported missing on the Eastern Front and her sister's husband had been killed, also on the Eastern Front. Also her house, in Halle, had been destroyed in one of the air raids and which is why she was living with Frau Edith.

The following day, before reporting to the Kommando, we visited the Cookhouse and scrounged as much food as we could carry and passed it onto the family as we could not help feeling sorry for them.

Wandering around we came across a farmhouse and caught a couple of chickens. For the first and only time, I managed to wring their necks. My method was not particularly scientific as, holding them by the head, I swung them around until their necks broke.

As with the birds of the previous day, the chickens were given to Frau Edith with the suggestion that they should be cooked for the evening meal.

Deciding it was time we reported to the Kommando we were delighted to find that we would be moving out the following morning and to ensure that we did not miss our transport it would be necessary to remain, that night, at the Kommando.

We returned to the billet and told Frau Edith that we were leaving Teutschental the following morning and that it was necessary to spend the night at the Kommando.

After the evening meal we said our farewells, the family were in tears at the amount of food we had given to them. As we cycled away, turning our heads we could see them waving their goodbyes.

Needless to say, it was a fairly sleepless night and we were up and about at the crack of dawn awaiting transport. This was arranged by the Americans and we were packed into the trucks so tightly it was only just possible to squeeze into a sitting a position. If we had had to stand on our heads we would not have objected, well not too much. We were on the next stage of the homeward trek and that was all that mattered.

The miles rolled by as we headed ever westwards, passing through village after village and crossing a river by pontoon bridge as the original had been destroyed.

Eventually we arrived at Nordhausen and were deposited at the airfield. As one would expect, the hangars were in ruins but holes in the runways had been repaired.

Having been split into parties of twenty-five, which was the pay-load for a Dakota, it was a case of waiting for a flight. As by now I would have received automatic promotion to Flight Sergeant, coupled with the fact that I was the sole senior NCO in the group, I decided to assume command.

Although Dakotas were landing fairly regularly they were reserved for wounded personnel. As the afternoon passed into evening and dusk began to fall, as the runway was without lighting, it became evident that there would be no further flights and we would be there overnight. Fortunately we were able to find shelter amid the ruined hangars and bedded down.

It was an uncomfortable night but the following morning, Friday, we were lucky as I was able to bag an aircraft and, without any delay, shepherded the group aboard. Chatting to the Pilot he was apologetic that we would have a bumpy ride due to adverse weather conditions over the Ruhr. As far as I was concerned I could not have cared less.

The door was closed, the engines started and revved up and we slowly taxied to the end of the runway. The green flare soared into the sky and the aircraft engines were revved up to maximum with the brakes hard on. The brakes were released and slowly we moved down the runway gradually gathering speed. The tail came up and after one or two bumps the wheels retracted and were locked in position.

We were airborne and gaining height as the Pilot went into a left hand turn to circle the airfield and set course on the next leg of the homeward trek.

One of the Scottish Paratroopers announced to all and sundry that flying was the proverbial piece of cake and there would be no need to worry if there were a few bumps. As to being airsick, that was completely out of the question. Needless to say, as the ride became bumpy he was the first to succumb and as there was not the luxury of air sickness bags his vomit spilled over the floor. Not a pleasant sight and the smell did not help either.

Although there were several bumps, to me there was nothing untoward. Naturally they were felt more in a Dakota as it was much smaller than the Halifax. I did wonder what the Pilot would have said, or done, if the turbulence had been such that the Dakota had been really thrown around. No doubt if the forecast had predicted heavy, or severe, turbulence we would have still been sitting on the ground at Nordhausen.

Apparently we should have landed at Brussels but for reasons not given we were diverted to Namur. At least we were no longer in Germany.

As soon as we had landed and taxied to the dispersal area we were loaded into trucks and whisked away to a Reception Centre. We were shepherded into the de-lousing chamber, all clothing taken away and, I understand, incinerated. At least we were not treated to dabs of disinfectant and our heads shaved as had happened at Stalag IVB.

We were kitted out from head to toe with American kit and surprise, surprise, issued with some Belgian francs. Feeling thoroughly clean I was ready to face the world and to carry on from where I had left off in 1943.

We were subjected to routine de-briefing which merely covered Number, Rank, Name, Service and the number of times that we had escaped. As regards my name I put Robert Leighton behind me and reverted to my true identity.

Since then I have often wondered what the reaction would have been if I had retained the identity of Robert Leighton until arriving in England and then quietly disappeared and re-appeared at 78 Squadron to announce I was Flight Sergeant Jack Sowter, ex-Stalag IVB.

After being shown to our billets we were free to wander around and take in the sights of Namur. But as far as I was concerned I was more interested in having a good night's sleep and so stayed put.

The next day was Saturday and, after breakfast, we were entrained to Ostend where it was 'goodbye' to the American Army and 'hello' to the British Army.

As our first meal was the inevitable Bully Beef the difference between British and American food was all too evident.

But being able to find the Sergeant's Mess I was able to make myself reasonably comfortable and it was a pleasant change to be able to listen to the wireless and read an English newspaper, even if the latter was several days old.

On the Sunday morning we were taken to the Docks and whilst in the Canteen waiting to embark I picked up a copy of *Lilliput*. One of the articles referred to a conversation which took place in Sweden between an American and a German civilian. The German said that he had lived in Hamburg until his home was destroyed in an air raid on the night of 27 July 1943 – the raid on which I was shot down.

For the crossing to England we embarked on a relatively small boat. Fortunately senior NCOs were allocated cabins but the Other Ranks, poor devils, were below deck close to the engines and the smell of oil.

As we sailed from Ostend in the early evening, I stood on deck watching the Port slowly disappear but only until it appeared to tilt from side to side and my stomach began to feel decidedly queasy.

Never having been happy on swings, I decided that enough was enough and disappeared back to my cabin and stretched out in the bunk. Despite the rough crossing I managed a reasonable night's sleep and escaped any sea-sickness.

Monday morning saw the boat anchored off Tilbury and I wondered how long we would have to wait before docking. Talking to some of the Other Ranks I learned that they had had a rotten crossing and that virtually all of them had been sea-sick.

As soon as we had disembarked the Red Cross provided breakfast of bacon and eggs and mugs of steaming hot tea. Telegram forms were issued for free messages home but I declined. I decided that I wanted my home-coming to be a surprise and not to be greeted with festoons of bunting and flag waving. From Tilbury we travelled to London Fenchurch Street by train and we were segregated into Army and Air Force.

After lunch we were given two hours to wander around Central London and I had the dubious honour of being arrested by two American MPs. However, although being dressed in American Army uniform, much to their disgust, my papers said who and what I was and not the GI who had gone AWOL as they had thought.

From Fenchurch Street railway station we were trucked to Paddington station and from there, by train, to Cosford in Shropshire. At the railway station more trucks were waiting to transport us to the nearby RAF Station.

After being shown our beds for the night we were given an evening meal which was followed by further form filling. We were given another 'free' telegram which I used to let my WAAF fiancee know that I was home.

One of the officers, obviously thinking I looked decidedly peaky, asked if I would like a couple of weeks at the Rehabilitation Centre at Scarborough. Although I was down to a mere eight stones, compared with my usual weight of ten and a half, I declined saying that I did not feel at all ill and that the lost weight would soon be recouped with some decent food.

That night I was far too excited to sleep and spent most of the night lying on the bed counting the hours and smoking.

The following day, Tuesday, we were kitted out and credentials were checked Although the Airman Clerk repeatedly referred to me as 'Sir', the reason why was not appreciated until he informed me that I had received two automatic promotions and that I was now a Warrant Officer. I had assumed that my rank was Flight Sergeant and so it became necessary to hurriedly change the rank badges on my uniform. Unfortunately, the uniform to go with the rank of Warrant Officer was not available.

Leave forms were completed, ration cards were issued and included sufficient points to allow for an initial period of double rations. Naturally we had no idea how the normal rations had been reduced. Most important of all we were provided with some money.

The remainder of the day we were left to our own desires as we were not due to go on Leave until the following day. This seemed almost like an anti-climax especially as there nothing to do and all day to fill.

On the Wednesday morning we were issued with Travel Warrants together with an itinerary of the trains and seat reservations.

With that completed we did not require a second bidding to collect our kit and assemble for the transport to the railway station.

My journey, such as it was, was from Cosford to Wolverhampton where it was necessary to cross from the GWR to the LMS station. Then onwards to Birmingham New Street with instructions to report to the RTO.

In the company of five others I boarded the Leeds train although I would be getting out at Burton-on-Trent. Talking between ourselves, one of them asked if I had noticed the picture above my head. To my amazement, by sheer coincidence it was a print of the castle ruins at Ashby-de-la-Zouch – my hometown.

At Burton-on-Trent I bade my travelling companions farewell and having several hours delay for a connecting train for the final nine miles, decided to take the bus. Walking across the town to the bus station I could smell the aroma of the beer being brewed and the small of hops seemed pretty good.

I caught the local 704 bus service to Ashby, and just after alighting bumped into my Uncle Bill on his way home to lunch. He took over my kit bag and we called at his house before popping over the road, to the Blue Bell, for a pint of Guinness.

As we crossed the road I saw my next door neighbour and asked if she would let Mum know I was home and that I would like bacon and egg for lunch. Needless to say, in the half an hour before reaching home the garden gate was adorned with bunting and flags and Mum was there to greet me.

At last, I was home and had kept my promise of always corning home even if I did have to walk. Well, in this case, part way. Now I could start to pick up the pieces and start, once again, living a normal life.

General Questionnaire for British/American Ex-Prisoners of War

In his questionnaire, Jack wrote a few words about his escape attempts and those of other incidents. The first is as follows:

PTE Vincent on the 15th of April 1944, kitted out a Pole of the German Army in British battledress for the purpose of the Pole returning to England as a member of the Free Polish Forces. This took place at Wallwitz.

Cpls Bluett & Smith and PTEs Kent & Thomas on the 25th of April 1945 at Wallwitz stole the bread ration for the Working Party for the following day and then left the Barrack to make their own way back to the West.

Of his own experiences, he wrote:

1st escape.

Stalag IVB. 17/8/44. By 'jumping' in the wood fatigue. 3 others escaped at the same time but moved from rendezvous before me. Recaptured 21/8/44.

2nd escape.

Stalag IVB. 23/8/44. Arrived IVB under escort of 2 guards, handed over to another guard for escort to search, delousing and being taken to the cells. Whilst at delousing, I joined a party going to hospital and escaped into the camp. I was employed for 2 days as cover for an escaped P.O.W. – F/SGT Colin Gray R.A.A.F. – after this I was wild in the camp until 30/8/44, when I escaped through the wire with R.S.M. Arthur Isherwood R.H.A., F/SGT Paul Marquet, Combined Ops and W.0.1 McClure R.C.A.F. We were recaptured on 8/9/44 at Lehrte by a railway official.

3rd attempt.

Stalag IVB. 4/4/45. By exchanging identity with PTE Ernest Leyton, Paratroop Regt., Service No.14224970, P.O.W. No. 90663, XIIA, to go out of working party at Wallwitz. Relieved by American forces 16/4/45.